Ladybird I'm Ready... to Spell!

Dictionary

Written by Angela Royston
and Miranda Irwin
Illustrated by Tom Heard

LADYBIRD BOOKS

UK | USA | Canada | Ireland | Australia
India | New Zealand | South Africa

Ladybird Books is part of the Penguin Random House group of companies
whose addresses can be found at global.penguinrandomhouse.com.

ladybird.com

First published 2015

001

Copyright © Ladybird Books Ltd 2015

Ladybird and the Ladybird logo are registered trademarks owned by Ladybird Books Ltd
The moral right of the author and illustrator has been asserted

Printed in China

A CIP catalogue record for this book is available from the British Library

ISBN: 978–0–723–29549–5

Contents

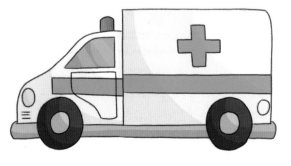

Using this dictionary

This dictionary will help you to:

• Check the spelling of words.

• Check the meaning of words.

• Find out about the grammar of words.

How to find a word in this dictionary:

• Write down the word, or think about how it is spelt.

• The words are arranged in alphabetical order. Look at the first letter of the word. Go to the section of the dictionary that covers that letter. Use the alphabet down the side of each page to help you find the right section.

• The words above the coloured line at the top of each set of two pages show you the first and last words on those pages.

• If you cannot find your word, check that you have spelt it correctly. Remember to take off word endings, such as 'ing' and 'ed', before looking for the word. If you still cannot find it, check at the back of the book, starting on page 110. Lots of common words are listed here. If it is not there either, you will need to look in a bigger dictionary.

• Sometimes two different words sound the same but are spelt differently. This dictionary uses the symbol ⚠ to remind you when this happens.

Reading this dictionary

(adj)
This word is an adjective. You can find out more about adjectives on page 108.

Some words have more than one meaning. Each number gives a different meaning.

This shows the first word on this page.

This shows the last word on this page.

All the words on the page start with this letter.

This shows how the plural of the noun is spelt.

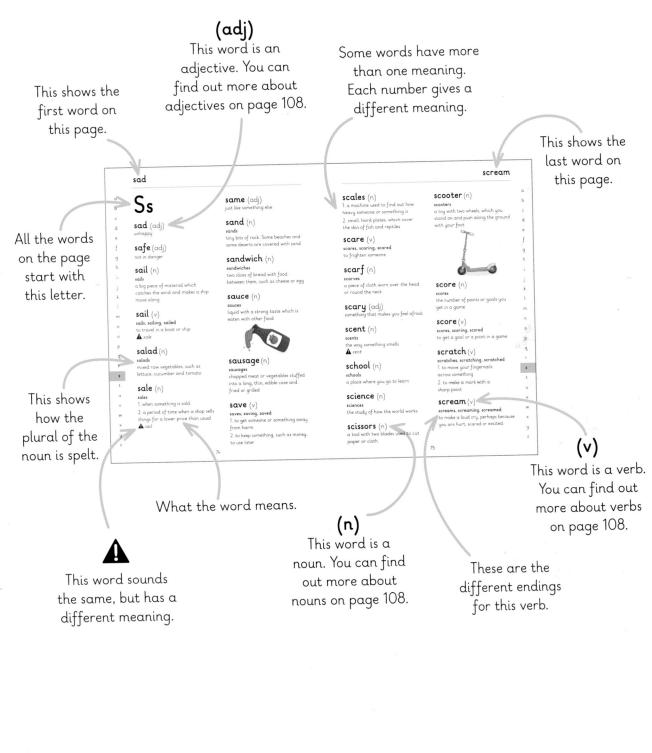

sad

Ss

sad (adj)
unhappy

safe (adj)
not in danger

sail (n)
sails
a big piece of material which catches the wind and makes a ship move along

sail (v)
sails, sailing, sailed
to travel in a boat or ship
⚠ sale

salad (n)
salads
mixed raw vegetables, such as lettuce, cucumber and tomato

sale (n)
sales
1. when something is sold
2. a period of time when a shop sells things for a lower price than usual
⚠ sail

same (adj)
just like something else

sand (n)
sands
tiny bits of rock. Some beaches and some deserts are covered with sand

sandwich (n)
sandwiches
two slices of bread with food between them, such as cheese or egg

sauce (n)
sauces
liquid with a strong taste which is eaten with other food

sausage (n)
sausages
chopped meat or vegetables stuffed into a long, thin, edible case and fried or grilled

save (v)
saves, saving, saved
1. to get someone or something away from harm
2. to keep something, such as money, to use later

scream

scales (n)
1. a machine used to find out how heavy someone or something is
2. small, hard plates, which cover the skin of fish and reptiles

scare (v)
scares, scaring, scared
to frighten someone

scarf (n)
scarves
a piece of cloth worn over the head or round the neck

scary (adj)
something that makes you feel afraid

scent (n)
scents
the way something smells
⚠ sent

school (n)
schools
a place where you go to learn

science (n)
sciences
the study of how the world works

scissors (n)
a tool with two blades used to cut paper or cloth

scooter (n)
scooters
a toy with two wheels, which you stand on and push along the ground with your foot

score (n)
scores
the number of points or goals you get in a game

score (v)
scores, scoring, scored
to get a goal or a point in a game

scratch (v)
scratches, scratching, scratched
1. to move your fingernails across something
2. to make a mark with a sharp point

scream (v)
screams, screaming, screamed
to make a loud cry, perhaps because you are hurt, scared or excited

This shows how the plural of the noun is spelt.

This shows the first word on this page.

All the words on the page start with this letter.

What the word means.

⚠
This word sounds the same, but has a different meaning.

(n)
This word is a noun. You can find out more about nouns on page 108.

These are the different endings for this verb.

(v)
This word is a verb. You can find out more about verbs on page 108.

Aa

abroad

to go or be in another country

absent (adj)

not here, away

accident (n)

accidents
getting hurt by chance

ache (n)

aches
(say *ake*) a pain that goes on
for a long time

across

on or to the other side

act (v)

acts, acting, acted
1. to pretend, play a part
2. to behave in a particular way

actually

really, as a matter of fact

add (v)

adds, adding, added
to put things together to make more

address (n)

addresses
a list that gives the number, street,
town and sometimes country of
a building

Dear Little Red Hen,
Sorry we did not
help you make the
bread. We promise
we will do so next
time.
Love Rat, Cat
and Dog

Little Red Hen
5 Acorn Road
Brambly Village

Fairyland

adult (n)

adults
a grown-up person or animal

adventure (n)

adventures
an exciting journey or outing

afraid (adj)

scared

again

once more

age (n)

ages
how old someone or something is

a
b
c
d
e
f
g
h
i
j
k
l
m
n
o
p
q
r
s
t
u
v
w
x
y
z

agree (v)

agrees, agreeing, agreed
to think the same as someone else

air (n)

the invisible gases we breathe in

airport (n)

airports
a place where aeroplanes land and take off

alarm (n)

alarms
a noise or signal made to get attention

alarm (v)

alarms, alarming, alarmed
to scare, frighten

alive (adj)

living

alone (adj)

on your own

alphabet (n)

alphabets
all the letters used to write the words of a language

altogether

completely, including everything or everyone

always

forever, at all times

amazing (adj)

wonderful, surprising

angel (n)

angels
1. a being with wings who is believed to come from heaven

2. an especially good or helpful person

angry (adj)

very cross

a
b
c
d
e
f
g
h
i
j
k
l
m
n
o
p
q
r
s
t
u
v
w
x
y
z

animal (n)

animals

a living thing that is not a plant. An animal can move about, breathe and eat *(see page 122)*

annoy (v)

annoys, annoying, annoyed

to make someone cross

another

1. one more

2. a different one

answer (v)

answers, answering, answered

to speak when someone asks you a question, or calls you

any

1. some of a larger amount, e.g. 'Do you have any pens?'

2. it doesn't matter which, e.g. 'Any pen will do.'

apologize (v)

apologizes, apologizing, apologized

to say sorry

appear (v)

appears, appearing, appeared

1. to come into sight

2. to seem

appetite (n)

appetites

liking for food

apron (n)

aprons

a piece of material that you wear over clothes to keep them clean

argue (v)

argues, arguing, argued

when two or more people talk about something they do not agree about

arithmetic (n)

a type of maths that uses numbers to add, subtract, multiply and divide

army (n)

armies

a large number of soldiers who are trained to fight together

arrive (v)

arrives, arriving, arrived
to reach a place

arrow (n)

arrows
1. a pointed stick that is shot from a bow
2. a sign that points in a particular direction

art (n)

a painting, drawing, statue or other work made by an artist

ask (v)

asks, asking, asked
to speak to someone to find the answer to a question, or to get something you want

asleep (adj)

when your eyes are shut and you are not aware of what is going on around you

athletics (n)

sports such as running and jumping

atlas (n)

atlases
a book of maps

attack (v)

attacks, attacking, attacked
to try to hurt someone or something

attention (n)

when you listen to and concentrate on what is going on around you

audience (n)

audiences
a crowd of people who listen to a concert or watch a play, film or other performance

automatic (adj)

1. happening without having to think
2. when a machine works by itself

autumn (n)

a season of the year *(see page 121)*

awake (adj)

not asleep

away

somewhere else

awful (adj)

horrible, nasty

a
b
c
d
e
f
g
h
i
j
k
l
m
n
o
p
q
r
s
t
u
v
w
x
y
z

a
b
c
d
e
f
g
h
i
j
k
l
m
n
o
p
q
r
s
t
u
v
w
x
y
z

Bb

baby (n)
babies
a very young child or animal

back (n)
backs
1. part of the body *(see page 114)*
2. the part farthest from the front *(see page 110)*

badge (n)
badges
a piece of plastic or metal with a picture or words, which you sew or pin to your clothes

bake (v)
bakes, baking, baked
to cook in an oven

balance (v)
balances, balancing, balanced
1. to place something so that it is steady and does not fall over
2. when two things have the same weight

ball (n)
balls
a sphere that you can kick, throw or hit, as part of a game or sport

ballet (n)
ballets
(say *bal-ay*) a type of dance that often tells a story

balloon (n)
balloons
a bag made of thin rubber, which you fill with air and use as a toy or decoration

band (n)
bands
1. a strip of cloth or rubber that you can put round something
2. a group of people playing musical instruments

bank (n)
banks
1. the ground alongside a river
2. a place where people keep their money

bark (n)
barks
1. a noise made by a dog
2. the layer of wood that covers the trunk and branches of a tree

bark (v)
barks, barking, barked
to make a short, loud noise like a dog

basket (n)
baskets
a container with handles for carrying or holding things. A basket is usually made of wire or the stems of plants woven together

bat (n)
bats
1. a piece of wood or metal used to hit a ball

2. a small, mouse-like animal with wings

bath (n)
baths
a long container that you can fill with water, usually to wash your body

bathroom (n)
bathrooms
a room that has a bath or a shower and a sink. Many bathrooms also have a toilet

battery (n)
batteries
an object filled with chemicals, which can make electricity

be (v)
is, being, was
to exist

beach (n)
beaches
sand or stones next to the sea

bean (n)
beans
seeds of some plants, which can be cooked and eaten
⚠ *been*

beat (v)
beats, beating, beat
1. to win against someone else
2. to hit many times with something

beautiful (adj)
lovely to look at or hear

a
b
c
d
e
f
g
h
i
j
k
l
m
n
o
p
q
r
s
t
u
v
w
x
y
z

because
the reason why

begin (v)
begins, beginning, began
to start *(see page 110)*

behave (v)
behaves, behaving, behaved
to act in a particular way

behaviour (n)
how you act

behind
at or to the back

believe (v)
believes, believing, believed
to think that something is true

bell (n)
bells
a piece of metal shaped like a cup
that rings when you hit or shake it

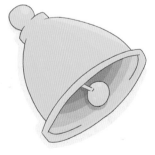

below
underneath, or at a lower level than
something *(see page 110)*

bench (n)
benches
a long, hard seat for more than one
person

bend (n)
bends
a curve in a path or object

bend (v)
bends, bending, bent
to change something's shape so that
it is no longer straight

bendy (adj)
able to bend easily

best (adj)
as good as possible, better than all
others

better (adj)
1. higher quality
2. no longer ill

bicycle (n)
bicycles
a vehicle that has two wheels and
pedals *(see page 116)*

bike (n)
bikes
bicycle or motorbike *(see page 116)*

birth (n)
births
the moment a baby is born

birthday (n)
birthdays
the day and month on which you were born

biscuit (n)
biscuits
a flat, baked food, usually sweet

bite (v)
bites, biting, bit
to use your teeth to cut something

blade (n)
blades
a flat piece of metal with a sharp edge for cutting. A knife has a blade

blind (adj)
unable to see

blood (n)
the red liquid that flows around inside your body

blow (v)
blows, blowing, blew
to make air move

board (n)
boards
a flat piece of material, which is hard and thin. Can be used for writing on (e.g. a whiteboard) or for playing board games

boat (n)
boats
a vehicle that carries people or things across water *(see page 116)*

body (n)
bodies
the whole of a person or animal *(see page 114)*

boil (v)
boils, boiling, boiled
1. when a liquid boils it becomes so hot it makes bubbles and steam
2. to cook food in boiling water

a b c d e f g h i j k l m n o p q r s t u v w x y z

bone (n)
bones

The hard pieces your skeleton is made of. Bones give your body its shape

bonfire (n)
bonfires

a fire that is made outdoors

book (n)
books

pages with words and/or pictures on them, held together inside a cover

boot (n)
boots

1. a kind of strong shoe that covers the lower leg as well as the foot

2. a place to carry things at the back of a car

born (adj)
came into the world

bottle (n)
bottles

a tall glass or plastic container used for holding liquid

bounce (v)
bounces, bouncing, bounced

to spring back after hitting a surface

bowl (n)
bowls

a round, hollow container that is open at the top

box (n)
boxes

a container made of cardboard, wood or plastic

boy (n)
boys

a child or young adult who is male

brake (n)
brakes

part of a bicycle, car or other vehicle which is used to stop the vehicle moving

⚠ *break*

brave (adj)
afraid of something scary but still able to act

bread (n)
a food made from flour and yeast

break (n)

breaks

a short rest

⚠ *brake*

break (v)

breaks, breaking, broke

1. when an object falls to pieces or stops working

2. to pull apart

⚠ *brake*

breakfast (n)

breakfasts

the first meal of the day

breathe (v)

breathes, breathing, breathed

to take air into and let air out of your body through your nose or your mouth

brick (n)

bricks

a block of hard material used for building *(see page 128)*

bridge (n)

bridges

a crossing built over a river, road or railway line

bright (adj)

very light or very colourful

brilliant (adj)

1. very bright

2. very good

bring (v)

brings, bringing, brought

to take something with you

broom (n)

brooms

a brush with a long handle for sweeping the ground

bruise (n)

bruises

an injury that makes your skin change from red to blue/black to yellow

brush (n)

brushes

a thing with many short, stiff hairs joined to a handle

a b c d e f g h i j k l m n o p q r s t u v w x y z

bubble (n)
bubbles
a small ball of liquid with air inside

bucket (n)
buckets
an open container with a handle, for carrying liquid or solids

build (v)
builds, building, built
to make something by putting different parts together

building (n)
buildings
a place that has walls and a roof

bump (n)
bumps
a lump or a rough part of something

bump (v)
bumps, bumping, bumped
to bang into something or someone

bun (n)
buns
1. a small cake or bread roll
2. a coil of hair at the back of your head

burst (v)
bursts, bursting, burst
when something splits and the air or liquid inside it pours out

busy (adj)
1. having a lot to do
2. when lots of people are at a place

butter (n)
a yellow, fatty food made by churning cream. Butter is spread on bread or used in cooking

button (n)
buttons
1. something you press to make something happen
2. a round, flat object used to fasten clothes

buy (v)
buys, buying, bought
to get something by paying money for it

Cc

café (n)
cafés
(say *caffay*) a kind of shop where you can sit down and eat or drink

cage (n)
cages
a box made of metal bars to prevent whatever is inside it from escaping

calculator (n)
calculators
a machine for doing sums

call (v)
calls, calling, called
1. to shout out
2. to telephone someone
3. to give someone or something a name

camera (n)
cameras
an object that takes photos or films

camp (v)
camps, camping, camped
to sleep in a tent or hut

capital (n)
capitals
1. a large letter, such as A, B or C
2. the main city of a country

card (n)
cards
1. stiff paper
2. stiff paper with a picture and words on it, given to people on special days, such as birthdays

cardboard (n)
thick, stiff paper *(see page 128)*

care (v)
cares, caring, cared
1. to look after
2. to think something is important

careful (adj)
thinking about what you are doing so that you do not make a mistake

carpet (n)
carpets
a soft covering for the floor

a
b
c
d
e
f
g
h
i
j
k
l
m
n
o
p
q
r
s
t
u
v
w
x
y
z

a
b
c
d
e
f
g
h
i
j
k
l
m
n
o
p
q
r
s
t
u
v
w
x
y
z

carry (v)

carries, carrying, carried
to move something from one place to
another

cartoon (n)

cartoons
1. a funny drawing
2. a film or story made using
funny drawings

castle (n)

castles
a large building with high, thick
walls. Castles were built long ago to
keep people safe

catch (v)

catches, catching, caught
to get hold of something that is
moving through the air

caterpillar (n)

caterpillars
a small, long animal with many legs.
All butterflies and moths begin life
as caterpillars

centre (n)

centres
the middle

cereal (n)

cereals
a breakfast food usually made from
corn, wheat, rice or oats

certain (adj)

sure

chain (n)

chains
a string of metal rings joined
together

chair (n)

chairs
a seat with a back for one person

chalk (n)

a piece of soft rock that can be used
for drawing or writing

chance (n)

chances
1. something that might happen,
or something that happens by luck
2. a risk. When you take a chance,
you hope something will happen,
but you cannot make it happen

change (n)

changes

1. when something is different from before
2. money given back to you when you pay too much

change (v)

changes, changing, changed

to become different or to make something different

chapter (n)

chapters

a part of a book

cheap (adj)

not costing a lot

cheat (v)

cheats, cheating, cheated

to break the rules in a game or exam

cheese (n)

cheeses

a food made from milk

child (n)

children

a young girl or boy, not yet an adult

chip (n)

chips

a fried stick of potato

chocolate (n)

chocolates

a sweet food made from cocoa

choose (v)

chooses, choosing, chose

to pick one thing rather than another

church (n)

churches

a building where Christians meet to pray

cinema (n)

cinemas

a building where films are shown on a large screen

circus (n)

circuses

a show, usually in a large tent, which may include clowns and acrobats

a
b
c
d
e
f
g
h
i
j
k
l
m
n
o
p
q
r
s
t
u
v
w
x
y
z

city (n)
cities
a large town where many people live and work

clap (v)
claps, clapping, clapped
to hit your hands together to make a noise

class (n)
classes
a group of children or adults learning with a teacher

clean (adj)
not dirty

clever (adj)
quick to learn

climb (v)
climbs, climbing, climbed
to move up something

clock (n)
clocks
an object that shows the time

close (v)
closes, closing, closed
to shut something

close (adj)
nearby

clothes (n)
things that people wear

cloud (n)
clouds
a white, grey or black shape in the sky. A cloud is made up of lots of tiny droplets of water

clown (n)
clowns
a person who dresses up in funny clothes and does silly things to make you laugh

club (n)
clubs
1. a group of people with the same interest
2. a stick used to hit something or someone

coat (n)

coats

1. a warm covering with sleeves, which you wear over your other clothes when you go outside

2. fur or hair that covers an animal's body

colour (n)

colours

the shade or tint of something *(see page 111)*

comic (n)

comics

a magazine with stories told in pictures

comic (adj)

funny

compare (v)

compares, comparing, compared

to look at two things to see how similar or different they are

compete (v)

competes, competing, competed

to take part in a race or contest

competitor (n)

competitors

a person who takes part in a race or contest

computer (n)

computers

an electronic machine that can remember large amounts of information, work out problems, and carry out lots of different tasks

concert (n)

concerts

a musical performance for an audience

consonant (n)

consonants

a letter of the alphabet that is not a vowel *(see page 100)*

container (n)

containers

something you can put things in

contest (n)

contests

an event in which people try to do something better than everyone else

control (v)

controls, controlling, controlled

to make something or someone do what you want

cook (v)

cooks, cooking, cooked

to heat food to make it ready to eat

a b **c** d e f g h i j k l m n o p q r s t u v w x y z

a
b
c
d
e
f
g
h
i
j
k
l
m
n
o
p
q
r
s
t
u
v
w
x
y
z

cool (adj)

1. a bit cold, but not very cold

2. fashionable or popular

copy (v)

copies, copying, copied

to make something that is the same as another thing

corner (n)

corners

where two roads, lines or sides meet

cost (n)

costs

what you pay for something

cot (n)

cots

a bed for a baby or small child

cough (v)

coughs, coughing, coughed

(say *kof*) to make a noise in your throat by suddenly pushing out air

count (v)

counts, counting, counted

1. to say numbers in order. If you count up to ten, you say all the numbers from one to ten

2. to find out how many things there are

country (n)

countries

1. a land with its own people and laws

2. land that is not a town or a city

cover (n)

covers

something that is put over or around something else

cover (v)

covers, covering, covered

to put one thing over or around another

crack (n)

cracks

a line or thin space in something

crane (n)

cranes

a machine for lifting heavy things high into the air

crash (n)

crashes

1. a loud noise
2. when two vehicles bang into each other

crash (v)

crashes, crashing, crashed

to hit something, producing a loud noise

creature (n)

creatures

an animal

cross (n)

crosses

the shape made by drawing one line across another

cross (v)

crosses, crossing, crossed

to go from one side to another

cross (adj)

annoyed about something

cry (v)

cries, crying, cried

to have tears coming from your eyes

cup (n)

cups

something with a handle that you drink from

cupboard (n)

cupboards

a box with a door for keeping things in

curly (adj)

not straight

a
b
c
d
e
f
g
h
i
j
k
l
m
n
o
p
q
r
s
t
u
v
w
x
y
z

a
b
c
d
e
f
g
h
i
j
k
l
m
n
o
p
q
r
s
t
u
v
w
x
y
z

curtain (n)

curtains

a piece of cloth that can be pulled across a window

curve (v)

curves, curving, curved

to bend smoothly

cushion (n)

cushions

a bag of soft material that you use to make a chair more comfortable

custard (n)

a sweet, yellow sauce made with milk and eggs, which is eaten with pudding

Dd

dance (n)

dances

steps or movements in time to music

dance (v)

dances, dancing, danced

to move in time to music

dangerous (adj)

not safe

dark (adj)

1. having no light or not much light

2. not pale (of colour)

date (n)

dates

1. a particular day, month and year

2. a sweet, brown, oval fruit

daughter (n)

daughters

a mother or father's female child

dead (adj)

no longer living

deaf (adj)

unable to hear

decorate (v)
decorates, decorating, decorated
to make something look pretty

delicious (adj)
tasting or smelling good

dentist (n)
dentists
someone who takes care of people's teeth

desk (n)
desks
a table you can work at

diagram (n)
diagrams
a picture that helps you to understand something

diamond (n)
diamonds
1. a hard, clear jewel
2. a shape with four sloping sides

diary (n)
diaries
1. a book for writing about what happens each day
2. a book for reminding you of events happening in the future

dictionary (n)
dictionaries
a book that tells you what words mean and how to spell them

die (n)
dice
a cube with one to six dots on each side. Dice are often used in games

different (adj)
not the same as something else

difficult (adj)
hard to do or understand

dig (v)
digs, digging, dug
to make a hole in the ground

dinner (n)
dinners
the main meal of the day

dinosaur

dinosaur (n)
dinosaurs
a type of reptile that lived a long time ago, and often reached an enormous size

direction (n)
directions
the way you are going or facing

dirty (adj)
covered with something that is not clean, such as mud

disappear (v)
disappears, disappearing, disappeared
to go out of sight

disappointed (adj)
sad because something you hoped for did not happen

discover (v)
discovers, discovering, discovered
to find or find out about something for the first time

disgusting (adj)
something that is sickening or horrible

distance (n)
distances
how far one thing is from another

dive (v)
dives, diving, dived
to jump into water head first

divide (v)
divides, dividing, divided
to split something up into smaller pieces or amounts

doctor (n)
doctors
someone who makes people better who are sick or hurt

doll (n)
dolls
a toy that looks like a small person

door (n)
doors
something that you open to get into a building, room or cupboard

dragon (n)
dragons
an animal in stories that breathes fire and has wings

draw (v)
draws, drawing, drew
1. to make a picture using a pencil, pen or crayon
2. to get the same score as the other team in a game or contest
⚠ *drawer*

drawer (n)
drawers
an open box you can keep things in, which slides in and out of a piece of furniture
⚠ *draw*

dream (n)
dreams
what you see and hear in your mind when you are asleep

dream (v)
dreams, dreaming, dreamt
to see and hear things in your mind when you are asleep

dress (n)
dresses
a piece of clothing for a girl or woman. It has a top and skirt joined together

dress (v)
dresses, dressing, dressed
to put on clothes

drink (n)
drinks
liquid that you swallow

drink (v)
drinks, drinking, drank
to swallow liquid

drive (v)
drives, driving, drove
to make a vehicle go from one place to another

dry (v)
dries, drying, dried
to get rid of all the water from something that is wet or damp

dry (adj)
not wet or damp

a
b
c
d
e
f
g
h
i
j
k
l
m
n
o
p
q
r
s
t
u
v
w
x
y
z

a
b
c
d
e
f
g
h
i
j
k
l
m
n
o
p
q
r
s
t
u
v
w
x
y
z

Ee

early (adj)
1. at the beginning of a period of time
2. before something starts. You might arrive early for school

earth (n)
soil, the stuff that plants grow in

Earth (n)
the planet we live on

easy (adj)
not hard to do or understand

eat (v)
eats, eating, ate
to chew and swallow food

ebook (n)
ebooks
a book that you read on a computer or tablet

edit (v)
edits, editing, edited
to alter or correct written words or film

elastic (n)
a material that stretches and then returns to its normal size

electricity (n)
a kind of energy that can be changed into heat and light and can make machines work

email (n)
emails
a message sent from one computer to another

empty (adj)
having nothing inside

end (v)
ends, ending, ended
to finish

energy (n)
the power to be able to do things

engine (n)
engines
a machine that uses energy to make something move. A car engine makes the car move

enjoy (v)
enjoys, enjoying, enjoyed
to like doing something

enough
(say *enuff*) as much as is needed

envelope (n)
envelopes
a container made of paper for a letter or card

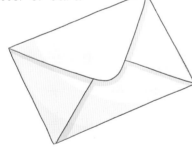

environment (n)
1. surroundings
2. everything about a place, including the land, air, water, plants, animals and people

equal (adj)
measuring the same as, or being worth the same as

escape (v)
escapes, escaping, escaped
to get away from something or someone

estimate (v)
estimates, estimating, estimated
to work out roughly, to guess

evening (n)
evenings
the time between the afternoon and the night

eventually
after a long time, in the end

every
everybody, everyone, everything, everywhere
each one, all

example (n)
examples
1. the way something should be done
2. one of a type to show what is meant

exciting (adj)
interesting and thrilling

a
b
c
d
e
f
g
h
i
j
k
l
m
n
o
p
q
r
s
t
u
v
w
x
y
z

exercise (n)

exercises

moving your body to keep it fit and healthy

exist (v)

exists, existing, existed

to be real

exit (n)

exits

the way out

expensive (adj)

costing a lot of money

explain (v)

explains, explaining, explained

to make something clear and easy to understand

Ff

face (n)

faces

the front of your head, including your eyes, nose and mouth

(see page 114)

fact (n)

facts

information that is true

factory (n)

factories

a building where machines are used to make something

fair (n)

fairs

a place to have fun, with stalls and rides

fair (adj)
treating people the same way or in a way that seems right

fairy (n)
fairies
in stories, a small, magical person with wings

fall (v)
falls, falling, fell
to drop to the ground, often by mistake

family (n)
families
a group of people who are related to each other. For example, grandparents, parents, brothers and sisters

famous (adj)
well known by a lot of people

fantastic (adj)
exciting or very good

farm (n)
farms
land used for growing plants and for keeping animals to sell for food

fat (n)
a soft substance that collects under the skin of people and other animals

fat (adj)
having more fat on your body than you need to be healthy

favourite (adj)
liked best

fear (n)
fears
the feeling of being scared

fearful (adj)
worried and scared

feather (n)
feathers
soft, light growths that cover a bird's body

feed (v)
feeds, feeding, fed
1. to give food to someone or something
2. to eat

a
b
c
d
e
f
g
h
i
j
k
l
m
n
o
p
q
r
s
t
u
v
w
x
y
z

31

a
b
c
d
e
f
g
h
i
j
k
l
m
n
o
p
q
r
s
t
u
v
w
x
y
z

feel (v)
feels, feeling, felt
1. to touch something to see what it is like
2. to have an emotion. For example, happy, sad, excited, angry

felt (n)
thick, woollen cloth

felt-tip (n)
felt-tips
a pen with a soft tip, which gives coloured ink

female (n)
females
a person or animal that can have babies or lay eggs, and is known as 'she'

fence (n)
fences
a kind of wall made of wood or metal poles

festival (n)
festivals
a special celebration, often to do with a religion. For example, Christmas is a Christian festival

few
not many, a small number of things

field (n)
fields
a large area of land surrounded by a fence, hedge or wall

fierce (adj)
when something looks or acts as though it's about to become angry or attack

fight (v)
fights, fighting, fought
when people or animals attack and hurt each other

fill (v)
fills, filling, filled
to put so much into a container that no more will fit in

film (n)
films
a series of moving pictures which tell a story

find (v)
finds, finding, found
to come across something

finish (v)
finishes, finishing, finished
to come to the end of something

fire (n)
fires
a pile of burning material

first (n)
number one, before all the others

fit (v)
fits, fitting, fitted
to be the right size

fit (adj)
healthy, particularly because of
doing excercise

fix (v)
fixes, fixing, fixed
to mend

flag (n)
flags
a piece of cloth with a pattern
on it. Every country and many
organizations have their own flag

flavour (n)
flavours
how something tastes

float (v)
floats, floating, floated
when something does not sink in
a liquid, or does not drop through
the air

flood (n)
floods
when water covers ground that is
usually dry

flour (n)
powder made from wheat or
other grains
⚠ *flower*

flower (n)
flowers
the part of a plant that makes seeds
(*see page 127*)
⚠ *flour*

a
b
c
d
e
f
g
h
i
j
k
l
m
n
o
p
q
r
s
t
u
v
w
x
y
z

fly

a
b
c
d
e
f
g
h
i
j
k
l
m
n
o
p
q
r
s
t
u
v
w
x
y
z

fly (n)
flies

a type of insect with wings

fly (v)
flies, flying, flew

to move through the air

fog (n)
a thick cloud close to the ground

fold (v)
folds, folding, folded

to bend paper or cloth so that one part lies over the other part

follow (v)
follows, following, followed

to go after something or someone

food (n)
what you eat

football (n)
1. a game in which two teams kick a ball and try to score a goal

2. footballs
the ball used to play football

forest (n)
forests

a large area of trees

forget (v)
forgets, forgetting, forgot

not remember something

fork (n)
forks

an object with a handle and three or four spikes, used for picking up food

fortune (n)
fortunes

a very large amount of money

forward
1. towards the front
2. to move in a direction ahead of you

frame (n)
frames

a border made by joining pieces of wood, plastic or metal together. A picture often has a frame round it

free (adj)
1. costing no money
2. able to do or say what you want, or to go where you want

freeze (v)
freezes, freezing, froze
to turn from liquid to solid. When water freezes it becomes ice

fridge (n)
fridges
a machine that keeps food cold

friend (n)
friends
someone you like and spend time with, and who likes you too

fright (n)
when something suddenly scares you

frighten (v)
frightens, frightening, frightened
to make a person or animal feel scared

front (n)
the farthest forward *(see page 100)*

fruit (n)
the sweet, juicy part of some plants. For example, strawberry or orange

fry (v)
fries, frying, fried
to cook in hot oil or fat

fuel (n)
fuels
something that is burnt to give heat or light, or to make something move. Petrol, gas and oil are fuels

full (adj)
unable to hold or contain any more

fun (n)
when you enjoy doing something and you feel happy

funny (adj)
1. when something makes you laugh
2. strange or odd

fur (n)
the thick hair that covers some animals

future (n)
the time that has yet to happen

a
b
c
d
e
f
g
h
i
j
k
l
m
n
o
p
q
r
s
t
u
v
w
x
y
z

a
b
c
d
e
f
g
h
i
j
k
l
m
n
o
p
q
r
s
t
u
v
w
x
y
z

Gg

game (n)
games
something you play that has rules. Chess and football are games

garage (n)
garages
1. a building or part of a house where a car is kept
2. a workshop where cars are mended
3. a place where drivers buy petrol or diesel

garden (n)
gardens
an area of land where plants are grown for people to enjoy

gas (n)
gases
something that is neither solid nor liquid. Air is a mixture of gases

gate (n)
gates
a type of door in a fence, hedge or wall

genius (n)
geniuses
an extremely clever person

gentle (adj)
careful and not rough

ghost (n)
ghosts
in stories, a person who is dead, but you can see or hear him or her

giant (n)
giants
a person in a story who is much taller than everyone else

giant (adj)
much bigger than usual

gift (n)
gifts
a present

girl (n)
girls
a child or young person who
is female

glass (n)
1. a hard, see-through material used
for windows, bottles and other things
(see page 128)

2. **glasses**
a type of cup made of glass

glasses (n)
a frame with two pieces of glass or
plastic, which help you to see better,
or which protect your eyes

gloomy (adj)
1. dark
2. sad, or not hopeful

glove (n)
gloves
a piece of clothing that covers
your hand

glue (n)
glues
a sticky substance that holds two
things together

glue (v)
glues, gluing, glued
to stick together with glue

goal (n)
goals
1. in some ball games, the place on
the field where the players have to
put the ball to score a point
2. a point scored by a player who
gets the ball in the goal

goblin (n)
goblins
an ugly imp or little monster
in a fairy story

gold (n)
a yellow precious metal that can be
used to make jewellery

good (adj)
1. something that you like or admire
2. well behaved, or well done

graph (n)
graphs
in maths, a picture that uses lines or
blocks to show information

a
b
c
d
e
f
g
h
i
j
k
l
m
n
o
p
q
r
s
t
u
v
w
x
y
z

a
b
c
d
e
f
g
h
i
j
k
l
m
n
o
p
q
r
s
t
u
v
w
x
y
z

grass (n)

grasses

a green plant with thin leaves. Grass is planted in parks and gardens to cover large areas

great (adj)

1. very large
2. very good
3. important

ground (n)

what you stand on outside

group (n)

groups

1. a number of people who share an activity. For example, a running group or a book group
2. lots of things or people in the same place. For example, a group of children

grow (v)

grows, growing, grew
to get bigger

grumpy (adj)

cross and not pleased with things

guess (v)

guesses, guessing, guessed
to say what you think might be the answer, though you are not sure

Hh

hair (n)

hairs

a long, thin strand that grows from your skin, particularly on your head *(see page 114)*

hairy (adj)

having lots of hair

half (n)

halves

one part of something that has been split into two equal parts

hall (n)

halls

1. a large room with lots of space, usually in a school, city or other public place
2. the space behind the front door in a house or flat

handle (n)
handles

the part of an object that you hold

happy (adj)
pleased, glad, content

hard (adj)
1. firm to the touch, not able
to be dented
2. difficult

hat (n)
hats

a piece of clothing that you wear on
your head

hate (v)
hates, hating, hated

to dislike something or someone very
much

have (v)
has, having, had

to hold or to own something

healthy (adj)
1. strong and not ill
2. something that helps to make you
strong and your body work well

hear (v)
hears, hearing, heard

to sense sounds with your ears

⚠ *here*

heat (v)
heats, heating, heated

to make warmer

height (n)
how high something is

help (v)
helps, helping, helped

to do something useful for someone

here
in this place

⚠ *hear*

hibernate (v)
hibernates, hibernating, hibernated

to spend winter in a deep sleep.
Bears and tortoises hibernate

hide (v)
hides, hiding, hid

to put something somewhere, or go
somewhere that no one can see

high (adj)
a long way above the ground

a
b
c
d
e
f
g
h
i
j
k
l
m
n
o
p
q
r
s
t
u
v
w
x
y
z

a
b
c
d
e
f
g
h
i
j
k
l
m
n
o
p
q
r
s
t
u
v
w
x
y
z

hill (n)
hills
ground that is higher than the land around it

hit (v)
hits, hitting, hit
to knock something or someone hard

hole (n)
holes
a space in the middle of something. For example, a sock may have a hole in it ⚠ *whole*

holiday (n)
holidays
1. time off from school or work
2. time spent staying somewhere away from home, for fun

hollow (adj)
empty inside

home (n)
homes
where you live

honest (adj)
telling the truth

hood (n)
hoods
a hat that is joined to a coat

hop (v)
hops, hopping, hopped
to jump on one leg

hope (v)
hopes, hoping, hoped
to want or expect something to happen

horrible (adj)
not nice

hospital (n)
hospitals
a building where doctors and nurses look after people who are ill or hurt

hot (adj)
very warm

house (n)
houses
a building, usually with more than one floor, where people live

hug (v)

hugs, hugging, hugged
to put your arms around someone or something and hold them tightly

huge (adj)
very large

human (n)
humans
a person

hungry (adj)
to feel the need to eat something

hurry (v)
hurries, hurrying, hurried
to go somewhere or do something quickly

hurt (v)
hurts, hurting, hurt
1. to feel pain
2. to make someone else feel pain

Ii

ice (n)
frozen water

ice cream (n)
ice creams
a frozen dessert made with cream, milk, eggs and sugar

idea (n)
ideas
a thought or opinion about something

ill (adj)
not well, sick

illness (n)
illnesses
when your body is not healthy

illustrator (n)
illustrators
someone who draws pictures for a book or magazine

imagine (v)
imagines, imagining, imagined
to make a picture in your mind

a
b
c
d
e
f
g
h
i
j
k
l
m
n
o
p
q
r
s
t
u
v
w
x
y
z

a
b
c
d
e
f
g
h
i
j
k
l
m
n
o
p
q
r
s
t
u
v
w
x
y
z

important (adj)

something or someone that matters a lot

impossible (adj)

something that cannot be done

in

1. surrounded by something else. For example, 'in the box'
2. at home
(see page 110)

information (n)

facts about something

injection (n)

injections

medicine that is pushed under the skin through a needle

ink (n)

the liquid inside a pen, which allows you to write or draw

insect (n)

insects

a small animal with six legs. Flies, ants and bees are all types of insect
(see page 126)

inside

1. the place within something
2. indoors *(see page 110)*

instead

in place of something or someone

instructions (n)

instruction

words and/or pictures that tell you how to do something

instrument (n)

instruments

1. something that you play to make music
2. a tool

interested (adj)

wanting to know about something

interesting (adj)

something that you enjoy doing or hearing about

internet (n)

a network of computers around the world, which can communicate with each other

interrupt (v)

interrupts, interrupting, interrupted
to stop someone when they are in the middle of doing or saying something

invite (v)

invites, inviting, invited
to ask someone to come to something, such as a party

iron (n)

irons
1. a tool that makes clothes smooth
2. a type of metal

island (n)

islands
land with water all around it

Jj

jacket (n)

jackets
a short coat

jam (n)

1. a spread made from fruit and sugar, which is often eaten on bread
2. traffic jam: when vehicles on the road move very slowly or not at all because something is blocking them

jar (n)

jars
a glass container with a lid

jealous (adj)

wanting what someone else has

jeans (n)

trousers made from denim

a
b
c
d
e
f
g
h
i
j
k
l
m
n
o
p
q
r
s
t
u
v
w
x
y
z

jelly (n)
jellies
a sweet dessert that wobbles

jet (n)
jets
a fast aeroplane

jewel (n)
jewels
a bright, shiny stone, used
in jewellery

jigsaw (n)
jigsaws
a puzzle made from a picture
cut into small pieces which you
fit together

job (n)
jobs
1. something a person is paid to do
2. a task that you have to do

joke (n)
jokes
something you say or do to make
people laugh

jug (n)
jugs
a container with a handle and a
spout for pouring liquid

juice (n)
juices
the liquid that comes out of fruit

jump (v)
jumps, jumping, jumped
to push off the ground into the air
with both feet

jungle (n)
jungles
a thick forest with lots of plants
and animals

Kk

keep (v)
keeps, keeping, kept
1. to save something for later
2. to carry on in the same way

kettle (n)
kettles
a closed pot with a handle and spout used for boiling water

key (n)
keys
1. a piece of metal that can turn a lock
2. a bar or button on a piano or keyboard, which you press to make a sound

kick (v)
kicks, kicking, kicked
to hit with your foot

kind (adj)
thoughtful and nice to other people

king (n)
kings
the male ruler of a country

kiss (v)
kisses, kissing, kissed
to touch with your lips

kitchen (n)
kitchens
a room where food is prepared

kite (n)
kites
a toy at the end of a long string, which flies in the air

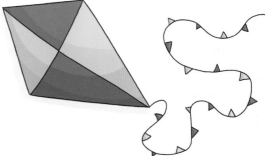

kneel (v)
kneels, kneeling, knelt
to go down on your knees

knife (n)
knives
an object with a blade used for cutting things

knight (n)
knights
a soldier who rode on horseback long ago

a
b
c
d
e
f
g
h
i
j
k
l
m
n
o
p
q
r
s
t
u
v
w
x
y
z

a
b
c
d
e
f
g
h
i
j
k
l
m
n
o
p
q
r
s
t
u
v
w
x
y
z

knot (n)

knots

something you make when you tie two pieces of rope or other material together

knot (v)

knots, knotting, knotted

to tie two ends or pieces of rope or other material together

know (v)

knows, knowing, knew

1. to understand and remember something
2. to remember someone you have met before

Ll

ladder (n)

ladders

a set of steps that can be moved from one place to another. A ladder is used to climb to high places

lady (n)

ladies

a polite word for a woman

lake (n)

lakes

a large pool of water with land all around it

land (n)

the parts of Earth's surface that are dry and not covered in water

land (v)

lands, landing, landed

when something that was in the air comes down to the ground

language (n)
languages
the words people use to speak and write to each other

lap (n)
laps
1. the flat surface made when you sit with your knees together
2. going once round a racetrack

lap (v)
laps, lapping, lapped
to drink using only the tongue, as a dog or cat does

laptop (n)
laptops
a computer that you can carry around with you and use on your lap

large (adj)
big

last (adj)
coming at the end, after all the others

late (adj)
when you arrive after you were supposed to

laugh (v)
laughs, laughing, laughed
to make a sound because you think something is funny or you are happy

law (n)
laws
a rule that people have to follow

lazy (adj)
not wanting to work

lead (v)
leads, leading, led
1. to go first
2. to show someone where to go or what to do

leaf (n)
leaves
the flat part of a tree or plant, which grows from a stem. Leaves are usually green (*see page 127*)

learn (v)
learns, learning, learnt
to get to know about something

a
b
c
d
e
f
g
h
i
j
k
l
m
n
o
p
q
r
s
t
u
v
w
x
y
z

a
b
c
d
e
f
g
h
i
j
k
l
m
n
o
p
q
r
s
t
u
v
w
x
y
z

least
the smallest amount

leave (v)
leaves, leaving, left
1. to go away from somewhere
2. to not take something with you

left (adj)
(see page 110)

length (n)
how long something is (see page 120)

less (adj)
not having as much as another person or thing

lesson (n)
lessons
when someone teaches you something, especially at school

letter (n)
letters
1. one of the signs we use to write words. There are twenty-six letters in the English alphabet
2. a message that you write to someone

library (n)
libraries
a building or room with lots of books which you can read or borrow

lick (v)
licks, licking, licked
to move your tongue over something

lie (v)
1. **lies, lying, lied**
to say something that you know is not true

2. **lies, lying, lay**
to rest on something with your body flat

life (n)
lives
the time when someone or something is alive

lift (n)
lifts
a machine that moves people or things from one floor to another in a building

lift (v)
lifts, lifting, lifted
to pick something up

light (n)
lights
a kind of energy that allows us to see the world. Light comes from the sun, fire and light bulbs

light (adj)
1. not dark
2. not heavy

lightning (n)
a flash of light in the sky when there is a thunderstorm

like (v)
likes, liking, liked
to think something or someone is good or nice

like (adj)
similar to something else

line (n)
lines
1. a long, thin mark
2. a row of people or things

lip (n)
lips
the outside edges of your mouth

liquid (n)
liquids
something wet that you can pour, such as water

list (n)
lists
things written down one after the other

listen (v)
listens, listening, listened
to hear something and think about it while you are hearing it

litter (n)
rubbish that is left lying around

little (adj)
small or smaller than other things

live (v)
lives, living, lived
1. to be alive
2. to have your home in a particular place

a
b
c
d
e
f
g
h
i
j
k
l
m
n
o
p
q
r
s
t
u
v
w
x
y
z

a
b
c
d
e
f
g
h
i
j
k
l
m
n
o
p
q
r
s
t
u
v
w
x
y
z

lock (n)

locks

something that keeps a door or box safely shut. A lock can be opened with a key that fits it

lock (v)

locks, locking, locked

to fasten a box or door so that it can only be opened with a key

lonely (adj)

unhappy because you are on your own

long (adj)

1. a great distance
2. taking a lot of time

look (v)

looks, looking, looked

to use your eyes to see something

lose (v)

loses, losing, lost
1. to be unable to find something
2. to not win a game or competition

loud (adj)

noisy

love (v)

loves, loving, loved

to have very strong and warm feelings for someone

lovely (adj)

very nice

low (adj)

near the ground

luck (n)

something good or bad that happens by chance

lucky (adj)

when something good happens by chance

lunch (n)

lunches

the meal in the middle of the day

Mm

machine (n)

machines

an object with different parts that work together to do a particular job

magic (n)

1. in stories, when something impossible happens
2. a clever trick which makes something happen that seems to be impossible

magnet (n)

magnets

a piece of metal that pulls things made of iron or steel towards it

mail (n)

letters and parcels sent by post

make (v)

makes, making, made

1. to create something new
2. to bring about an event by saying or doing something

male (n)

males

a boy, man or any person or animal known as 'he'

man (n)

men

a grown-up male

many (adj)

a lot of something

map (n)

maps

a drawing of a place seen from above

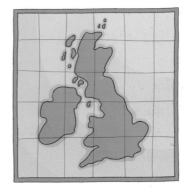

mark (n)

marks

1. a shape or sign, such as a tick, drawn on paper or another surface
2. a line or spot on something which is not supposed to be there
3. the number of correct answers out of the total

a b c d e f g h i j k l m n o p q r s t u v w x y z

mark (v)

marks, marking, marked

when a teacher checks written work and corrects it

market (n)

markets

a group of stalls where people go to buy and sell things

marry (v)

marries, marrying, married

to become the husband or wife of someone

mat (n)

mats

a thick piece of material that covers part of a floor or table

match (n)

matches

1. something that goes with something else exactly

2. a game between two people or teams

3. a special stick which makes a flame when rubbed against something rough

material (n)

materials

what something is made of. Wood, metal and plastic are different types of material *(see page 128)*

meal (n)

meals

food you sit down to eat at about the same time every day, such as breakfast or dinner

measure (v)

measures, measuring, measured

to find the size of something *(see page 120)*

meat (n)

food that comes from animals that have been killed

⚠ *meet*

medicine (n)

medicines

something you take to help you feel better when you are ill

meet (v)

meets, meeting, met

1. to get together with other people

2. to come across someone you know

⚠ *meat*

melt (v)
melts, melting, melted
1. to warm a solid until it turns into a liquid
2. to turn from a solid into a liquid

memory (n)
memories
something that happened to you in the past and which you remember

mess (n)
an untidy or dirty muddle

message (n)
messages
something you write or say, which gives information

messy (adj)
untidy or dirty

metal (n)
metals
a hard, shiny material, such as iron, gold or silver

microphone (n)
microphones
a electric machine that picks up sound so it can then be made louder or recorded

middle (n)
the centre of something

might
when something is possible or may happen

milk (n)
a white liquid which comes from mothers to feed their babies. People often drink cows' milk

mind (n)
minds
the part of you that thinks, feels and remembers

mind (v)
minds, minding, minded
to care about something

mirror (n)
mirrors
a special piece of glass in which you can see yourself

miss (v)
misses, missing, missed
1. to not get something that you tried to get
2. to feel sad because someone or something is not there

a
b
c
d
e
f
g
h
i
j
k
l
m
n
o
p
q
r
s
t
u
v
w
x
y
z

mistake (n)

mistakes

something that is wrong by accident

mix (v)

mixes, mixing, mixed

to put things together and stir them around

mobile (n)

mobiles

1. a phone that you carry around with you

2. a hanging toy, usually for a baby

model (n)

models

1. a small copy of something

2. a person who wears clothes and shoes to show what they look like

money (n)

what we use to pay for things

monster (n)

monsters

a scary creature in stories

month (n)

months

a part of the year, about four weeks long *(see page 117)*

moon (n)

moons

a large, natural object that circles round a planet

Moon (n)

the large object that circles the Earth. It is the brightest thing we see in the sky at night

more

a bigger amount

morning (n)

mornings

the time from the beginning of the day until the middle of the day

mosque (n)

mosques

(say *mosk*) a building where Muslims meet to pray

most
almost all

mother (n)
mothers
a woman who has a son or daughter

mountain (n)
mountains
a very high hill

mouth (n)
mouths
the part of your face that includes your lips, teeth and tongue
(see page 114)

move (v)
moves, moving, moved
1. to go from one place to another
2. to take something from one place to another

mud (n)
wet soil

music (n)
the sound made by someone singing or playing an instrument

must
when someone has to do something

Nn

nail (n)
nails
1. the hard covering at the end of each of your fingers and toes
2. a small piece of metal with a pointy end used to join pieces of wood together

name (n)
names
what something or someone is called

nasty (adj)
not at all nice, horrible

nature (n)
everything in the world that has not been made by people

naughty (adj)
doing things that are bad or not allowed

near (n)
close to

neat (adj)
tidy and not in a mess

a
b
c
d
e
f
g
h
i
j
k
l
m
n
o
p
q
r
s
t
u
v
w
x
y
z

a
b
c
d
e
f
g
h
i
j
k
l
m
n
o
p
q
r
s
t
u
v
w
x
y
z

necklace (n)
necklaces
jewellery worn round your neck

need (v)
needs, needing, needed
when you must have something

neighbour (n)
neighbours
someone who lives next door
or near you

nervous (adj)
worried about something that is
happening or going to happen

nest (n)
nests
a home built by birds and
some animals

new (adj)
1. just bought, not used before
2. fresh, something you have not
seen, heard or done before

news (n)
information about what is
happening

next (adj)
1. the one after this one
2. the one nearest to you

nice (adj)
someone who is kind and pleasant, or
something that makes you feel good

night (n)
nights
the time when it is dark because the
sun has set

nightmare (n)
nightmares
a scary dream

noise (n)
noises
a loud sound or sounds

noisy (adj)
making a lot of loud sounds

none (n)
not any

note (n)
notes
1. a short letter
2. one musical sound

now (n)
at this time

number (n)
numbers
a word or symbol that tells you how many of something there are
(see page 119)

nurse (n)
nurses
someone who looks after people who are sick or hurt

Oo

object (n)
objects
a solid thing

ocean (n)
oceans
a very big sea

odd (adj)
1. different, strange
2. numbers that cannot be shared into two equal amounts

oil (n)
1. a black liquid which is found under the ground. Oil is burnt to give energy for heating and to make electricity. It is also burnt as petrol in vehicles to make them go
2. a liquid made from some plants, such as olives, which is used for cooking

old (adj)
1. a person or animal that has lived for a long time
2. made a long time ago

a
b
c
d
e
f
g
h
i
j
k
l
m
n
o
p
q
r
s
t
u
v
w
x
y
z

once

once
1. something that happened some time ago
2. something that happens one time only

only
1. no more than. For example, 'She had only one shoe.'
2. No longer than. For example, 'The holiday lasted only three days.'

open (adj)
not closed or blocked

opposite (n)
opposites
as different as possible to something

order (v)
orders, ordering, ordered
1. to tell someone that they must do something
2. to ask for something that you want to buy
3. to arrange things in a certain way

ordinary (adj)
normal or usual

other (n)
others
a different one

out
1. in the open air
2. not at home
(see page 110)

outdoors (n)
outside in the open air

outside
1. the surface of something
2. in the open air *(see page 110)*

oven (n)
ovens
a box or machine in which air is made hot so that it can cook or heat food

overweight (adj)
weighing too much

own (v)
owns, owning, owned
to have something that is yours

Pp

packet (n)
packets
a cardboard box or paper or plastic wrapping which you can put things in

page (n)
pages
one side of a piece of paper in a book

pain (n)
pains
the feeling you have when part of your body hurts

paint (n)
paints
a thick, coloured liquid, used to colour a picture, wall or other surface

paint (v)
paints, painting, painted
1. to make a picture with paints
2. to cover something with paint

pair (n)
pairs
two things that go together. For example, you wear a pair of socks

palace (n)
palaces
a very grand home for a king or queen and their family

pale (adj)
with little colour

pancake (n)
pancakes
a thin cake made from eggs, milk and flour and fried in a pan

pantomime (n)
pantomimes
a funny play with songs. Pantomimes often tell fairy stories, and are usually performed around Christmas time

paper (n)
papers
a thin material made from wood and used for writing and drawing on (see page 128)

park (n)
parks
a large, public garden where people can walk and enjoy themselves

a
b
c
d
e
f
g
h
i
j
k
l
m
n
o
p
q
r
s
t
u
v
w
x
y
z

a
b
c
d
e
f
g
h
i
j
k
l
m
n
o
p
q
r
s
t
u
v
w
x
y
z

park (v)
parks, parking, parked
to stop a vehicle and leave it – usually in a car park or at the side of the road

part (n)
parts
a piece of something

particularly
especially

partner (n)
partners
someone who does things with you

party (n)
parties
an event where people come together to have fun

pass (v)
passes, passing, passed
1. to put something into someone else's hand
2. to go by something or someone
3. to do well enough in a test

past (n)
the time before now

paste (n)
a thick, wet mixture

path (n)
paths
a strip of ground that you can walk along

patient (n)
patients
someone who is being cared for because they are ill or hurt

patient (adj)
able to wait for something, or to try hard to do something difficult without getting angry

pattern (n)
patterns
a group of numbers, pictures or shapes which are repeated again and again

paw (n)
paws
an animal's foot, with claws and soft pads

pay (v)
pays, paying, paid
to give money for something

peace (n)
when things are quiet, still and calm
⚠ *piece*

pedal (n)
pedals
something you press with your foot
to make a machine work

pedal (v)
pedals, pedalling, pedalled
to make a machine go by moving
the pedals

peg (n)
pegs
1. a hook for hanging coats
2. a clip for holding washing
on a line

pen (n)
pens
what you use to write in ink

pencil (n)
pencils
a thin wooden stick with black or
coloured material inside it which you
use to write or draw

penny (n)
pennies or pence
a small coin. 100 pennies make a
British pound

perfect (adj)
so good, it couldn't be any better

perform (v)
performs, performing, performed
to act, sing or dance in front of an
audience

performance (n)
performances
a play, dance or other activity done
in front of an audience

perhaps
maybe, something that might or
might not happen

person (n)
people or persons
a man, woman or child

a
b
c
d
e
f
g
h
i
j
k
l
m
n
o
p
q
r
s
t
u
v
w
x
y
z

pet

a
b
c
d
e
f
g
h
i
j
k
l
m
n
o
p
q
r
s
t
u
v
w
x
y
z

pet (n)
pets

an animal you keep and look after in your home

phone (n)
phones

short for telephone. A machine you use to talk to someone who is somewhere else

photo (n)
photos

short for photograph. A picture taken with a camera

piano (n)
pianos

a large instrument with black and white keys that you press to make music

picnic (n)
picnics

a meal eaten outside

picture (n)
pictures

a painting, drawing or photograph

piece (n)
pieces

a part of something bigger

⚠ *peace*

pile (n)
piles

things put on top of each other

pillow (n)
pillows

something large and soft that you rest your head on in bed

pirate (n)
pirates

a person who attacks ships at sea and steals things from them

pizza (n)
pizzas

a type of food made by putting tomatoes, cheese and other toppings on a type of bread base

place (n)
places
1. where something goes or belongs
2. an area with a name, such as a town or wood

plain (adj)
simple, not decorated

planet (n)
planets
a large object in space which moves round a star. For example, Earth, Mars and Jupiter are planets that move round the Sun

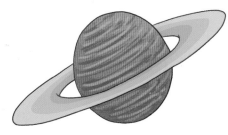

plant (n)
plants
a living thing with leaves, which makes seeds. Most plants grow from a seed in the ground *(see page 127)*

plaster (n)
plasters
material stuck over a cut to keep it clean

plastic (n)
a material made from oil. Plastic is used to make bottles, toys, bags and many other things *(see page 128)*

plate (n)
plates
a round, flat object you put food on

play (n)
plays
a story performed by actors

play (v)
plays, playing, played
1. to do something for fun
2. to take part in a game or sport
3. to make sounds with an instrument

playground (n)
playgrounds
an outside space for children to play in

please
a word used to ask for something politely

pleased (adj)
happy about something

a b c d e f g h i j k l m n o **p** q r s t u v w x y z

pocket

a
b
c
d
e
f
g
h
i
j
k
l
m
n
o
p
q
r
s
t
u
v
w
x
y
z

pocket (n)

pockets

a pouch sewn on to clothes for putting things in

poem (n)

poems

a piece of writing where the words are chosen for how they sound as well as what they mean. Poems often rhyme

point (n)

points

the sharp end of something such as a needle

point (v)

points, pointing, pointed

to show where something is by stretching your finger out towards it

police (n)

men and women whose job it is to stop others from breaking the law, and to make sure people are safe

polite (adj)

having good manners, not being rude

pond (n)

ponds

a pool of water with plants and animals, often in a garden or a park

pool (n)

pools

an area of still water

poor (adj)

not having enough money

possible (adj)

could happen

post (n)

posts

1. a pole fixed in the ground. For example, a goal post
2. a system of sending letters and parcels by paying a company to deliver them

post (v)

posts, posting, posted

to put a letter or parcel in a letterbox or take it to a post office so it can be sent from one person to another

poster (n)
posters
a large picture or notice on the wall

pound (n)
pounds
100 pennies make a British pound.
One pound is written as £1

pour (v)
pours, pouring, poured
to make liquid run out of something
such as a jug or a kettle

powder (n)
powders
tiny bits of something. For example,
salt is a powder

power (n)
1. strength, energy
2. being able to control other people
3. a magical or special ability

precious (adj)
very special or valuable

prepare (v)
prepares, preparing, prepared
to get ready

present (n)
1. the time right now
2. **presents**
a gift

pretend (v)
pretends, pretending, pretended
to act like something is true when it
is not

pretty (adj)
nice to look at

price (n)
prices
the amount of money you have to
pay for something

prince (n)
princes
the son of a king or queen

princess (n)
princesses
the daughter of a king or queen

prize (n)
prizes
something you get for winning

a
b
c
d
e
f
g
h
i
j
k
l
m
n
o
p
q
r
s
t
u
v
w
x
y
z

problem (n)
problems
1. something difficult
2. something that is hard to do anything about

programme (n)
programmes
a show on radio or television

promise (v)
promises, promising, promised
to tell someone that you will definitely do or not do something

pudding (n)
puddings
something sweet which you eat after a meal

puddle (n)
puddles
a small pool of water, often found after it has rained

pull (v)
pulls, pulling, pulled
to take hold of something and move it towards you. The opposite of push *(see page 110)*

pupil (n)
pupils
1. someone being taught
2. the small black dot in the centre of your eye

puppet (n)
puppets
a doll that you can make move, such as by pulling strings or moving your hand

purse (n)
purses
a small bag for keeping money in

push (v)
pushes, pushing, pushed
to take hold of something and move it away from you.
The opposite of pull *(see page 110)*

puzzle (n)
puzzles
a game or problem that is hard to work out

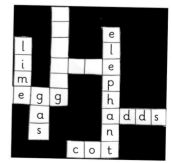

Qq

quality (n)
how well something is made

quantity (n)
quantities
how much there is or how many there are

quarrel (n)
quarrels
an argument between two people who are angry with each other

quarter (n)
quarters
one of four equal parts of something

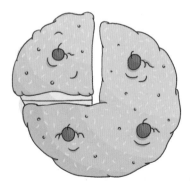

queen (n)
queens
1. the female ruler of a country
2. the wife of the king

question (n)
questions
what you ask when you want to find out something

queue (n)
queues
a line of people or cars waiting for something. The one at the front of the queue goes first, and the one at the back goes last

quick (adj)
fast

quiet (adj)
with little or no noise

quite
1. fairly. For example, 'I am quite good at tennis.'
2. completely. For example, 'Are you quite sure?'

quiz (n)
quizzes
1. a series of questions, often on the same topic
2. a contest in which people compete to answer questions

Rr

race (n)
races
a contest to find out who is the fastest

racket (n)
rackets
1. a type of sports bat which has strings stretched across an oval frame
2. a loud noise

radiator (n)
radiators
a metal object that is used to heat a room

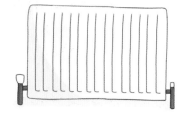

radio (n)
radios
a machine that allows you to hear music, news and other programmes sent from a radio station

railway (n)
railways
a metal track that trains move along

rain (n)
drops of water that fall from clouds in the sky

rainbow (n)
rainbows
bands of colour which form an arch in the sky when it is sunny and raining at the same time

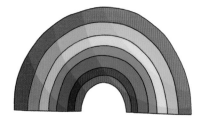

rare (adj)
unusual, uncommon

rattle (n)
rattles
an object that makes a noise when it is shaken

rattle (v)
rattles, rattling, rattled
to shake something so that it makes a noise

reach (v)
reaches, reaching, reached
1. to get to a place
2. to stretch your arm to get something

read (v)
reads, reading, read
to understand the meaning of written words

ready (adj)
able to be used now, or able to do something now

real (adj)
something that is true and is not made up

really
truly

reason (n)
reasons
why something happens, or why someone does something

recipe (n)
recipes
a list of the things you need to cook something, and instructions telling you how to cook it

record (n)
records
1. information about an event which is written down and kept
2. the best so far

record (v)
records, recording, recorded
1. to write down information
2. to use a machine to make a copy of sounds or a television programme

recorder (n)
recorders
a musical instrument that you blow into to make a sound

referee (n)
referees
a person who makes sure that players in a game follow the rules

reflection (n)
reflections
what you see when you look in a mirror

refuse (v)
refuses, refusing, refused
to say 'no' to something

register (n)
registers
a list of names

a
b
c
d
e
f
g
h
i
j
k
l
m
n
o
p
q
r
s
t
u
v
w
x
y
z

a
b
c
d
e
f
g
h
i
j
k
l
m
n
o
p
q
r
s
t
u
v
w
x
y
z

register (v)
registers, registering, registered
to put your name down to take part in something

relative (n)
relatives
a member of your family

religion (n)
religions
the belief in a god or gods, with particular ideas and customs that lots of people follow

remember (v)
remembers, remembering, remembered
to bring into your mind something you know or that happened in the past

remind (v)
reminds, reminding, reminded
to help someone to remember something

remove (v)
removes, removing, removed
to take something away

repair (v)
repairs, repairing, repaired
to mend

reply (v)
replies, replying, replied
to give an answer or to respond

rescue (v)
rescues, rescuing, rescued
to save from danger or harm

rest (n)
1. a break from doing something
2. the remaining part of something

rest (v)
rests, resting, rested
1. to stop doing something for a while
2. to sit or lie down when you are tired

restaurant (n)
restaurants
a place where people can buy and eat a meal

return (v)

returns, returning, returned

1. to come or go back
2. to give something back

rhyme (v)

rhymes, rhyming, rhymed

when a word has the same sound at the end as another word. For example, 'ball' and 'fall' rhyme

rhythm (n)

rhythms

a repeated pattern of beats

ribbon (n)

ribbons

a strip of coloured fabric

rice (n)

a grain that is grown mostly in Asia, and is a very popular food around the world

rich (adj)

having a lot of money

ride (v)

rides, riding, rode

to travel on something; for example, a bike or a horse

right (adj)

1. correct
2. the opposite of left (*see page 110*)
⚠ *write*

ring (n)

rings

1. a round band that you wear on your finger
2. the sound of a bell

ring (v)

rings, ringing, rang

1. to make the sound of a bell
2. to call someone on the phone

ripe (adj)

when a fruit is soft and ready to eat

rise (v)

rises, rising, rose

to go up

river (n)

rivers

a long stretch of water which flows across the land to the sea or a lake

a
b
c
d
e
f
g
h
i
j
k
l
m
n
o
p
q
r
s
t
u
v
w
x
y
z

road (n)

roads

a long stretch of hard ground for vehicles to travel along

roar (v)

roars, roaring, roared

to make a sound like a lion

robot (n)

robots

a machine that can do a particular job by itself. A robot is controlled by a computer

rock (n)

rocks

a hard, rough material

rock (v)

rocks, rocking, rocked

to move gently from side to side

rocket (n)

rockets

1. a type of engine that is used to lift a spacecraft from the ground into space

2. a type of firework

roll (n)

rolls

1. a long strip of tape, paper or other material which is wound round a tube

2. a small, round loaf of bread, often used to make a sandwich

roll (v)

rolls, rolling, rolled

to turn over and over, moving across the ground

roof (n)

roofs

the hard top of a building

room (n)

rooms

a space inside a building with its own walls, floor, ceiling and door

root (n)

roots

the part of a plant that grows in the ground (see page 127)

rope (n)

ropes

a long piece of material made up of lots of strands twisted together

rough (adj)

bumpy, not smooth

round (adj)

shaped like a ball or a circle

row (n)

rows

1. a line of people or things
(rhymes with 'low')

2. an angry argument
(rhymes with 'now')

row (v)

rows, rowing, rowed

1. to move a boat, using oars
(rhymes with 'low')

2. to have an angry argument
(rhymes with 'now')

rubber (n)

rubbers

1. a soft, bendy material

2. a device for getting rid of pencil
marks

rubbish (n)

things thrown away

rude (adj)

being cheeky and unpleasant,
not polite

rule (n)

rules

a list of what you can and cannot
do. For example, schools have rules
and so do games

rule (v)

rules, ruling, ruled

to be in charge of all the people in a
country

ruler (n)

rulers

1. a straight piece of plastic, metal
or wood used to measure how long
something is

2. someone who runs a country

run (v)

runs, running, ran

to move faster than walking, with
only one foot on the ground at a
time

a
b
c
d
e
f
g
h
i
j
k
l
m
n
o
p
q
r
s
t
u
v
w
x
y
z

Ss

sad (adj)
unhappy

safe (adj)
not in danger

sail (n)
sails

a big piece of material which catches the wind and makes a ship move along

⚠ *sale*

sail (v)
sails, sailing, sailed

to travel in a boat or ship

salad (n)
salads

mixed raw vegetables, such as lettuce, cucumber and tomato

sale (n)
sales

1. when something is sold

2. a period of time when a shop sells things for a lower price than usual

⚠ *sail*

same (adj)
just like something else

sand (n)
sands

tiny bits of rock. Some beaches and some deserts are covered with sand

sandwich (n)
sandwiches

two slices of bread with food between them, such as cheese or egg

sauce (n)
sauces

liquid with a strong taste, which is eaten with other food

sausage (n)
sausages

chopped meat or vegetables stuffed into a long, thin, edible case and fried or grilled

save (v)
saves, saving, saved

1. to get someone or something away from harm

2. to keep something, such as money, to use later

scales (n)

1. a machine used to find out how heavy someone or something is

2. small, hard plates, which cover the skin of fish and reptiles

scare (v)

scares, scaring, scared
to frighten someone

scarf (n)

scarves
a piece of cloth worn over the head or round the neck

scary (adj)

something that makes you feel afraid

scent (n)

scents
the way something smells

⚠️ *sent*

school (n)

schools
a place where you go to learn

science (n)

sciences
the study of how the world works

scissors (n)

a tool with two blades used to cut paper or cloth

scooter (n)

scooters
a toy with two wheels, which you stand on and push along the ground with your foot

score (n)

scores
the number of points or goals you get in a game

score (v)

scores, scoring, scored
to get a goal or a point in a game

scratch (v)

scratches, scratching, scratched

1. to move your fingernails across something

2. to make a mark with a sharp point

scream (v)

screams, screaming, screamed
to make a loud cry, perhaps because you are hurt, scared or excited

a
b
c
d
e
f
g
h
i
j
k
l
m
n
o
p
q
r
s
t
u
v
w
x
y
z

sea

a
b
c
d
e
f
g
h
i
j
k
l
m
n
o
p
q
r
s
t
u
v
w
x
y
z

sea (n)

seas

a huge area of salty water

⚠ *see*

search (v)

searches, searching, searched

to look for something

seaside (n)

the land that is next to the sea

season (n)

seasons

part of the year when the weather, plants and animals do certain things *(see page 121)*

seat (n)

seats

something to sit on

seatbelt (n)

seatbelts

a band of fabric that is fixed to the seat of a car, bus or aircraft. The seatbelt clips over your body and helps to keep you safe

second (n)

1. **seconds**

a short length of time – the time it takes for a clock to make one tick

2. the one after first *(see page 119)*

secret (n)

secrets

something that you do not want most people to know

see (v)

sees, seeing, saw

to be aware of something with your eyes

⚠ *sea*

seed (n)

seeds

the part of a plant that can grow into a new plant

sell (v)

sells, selling, sold

to give something to someone in exchange for money

send (v)

sends, sending, sent

to make someone or something go somewhere

sense (n)

senses

1. knowing what is going on around you. You have five senses – seeing, hearing, feeling, smelling and tasting

2. what seems right. Something makes sense when it seems right or you understand it

sensible (adj)

good at knowing the wisest thing to do

sentence (n)

sentences

1. a group of words that make sense together

2. the punishment you get if you break the law

separate (adj)

not joined together

serious (adj)

important, not to be laughed at

settee (n)

settees

a soft seat for two or more people. Also known as a sofa or couch

sew (v)

sews, sewing, sewed

to join two pieces of cloth together using a needle and thread

⚠ *so, sow*

shadow (n)

shadows

a dark shape made by something that blocks out a bright light

shake (v)

shakes, shaking, shook

to move something quickly from side to side or up and down

shallow (adj)

not deep (*see page 110*)

shampoo (n)

a liquid with soap in it used for washing hair

shape (n)

shapes

the outline of an object
(*see page 118*)

a
b
c
d
e
f
g
h
i
j
k
l
m
n
o
p
q
r
s
t
u
v
w
x
y
z

a
b
c
d
e
f
g
h
i
j
k
l
m
n
o
p
q
r
s
t
u
v
w
x
y
z

share (v)
shares, sharing, shared
to give or lend something you have
to another person

sharp (adj)
able to cut

shed (n)
sheds
a small hut for keeping things in,
often in the garden

sheet (n)
sheets
1. a large piece of cloth which covers
your bed and is next to your skin
2. a piece of paper

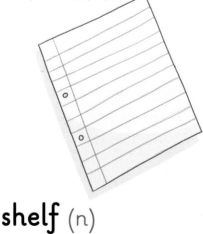

shelf (n)
shelves
a long, flat piece of wood or other
material, attached to a wall and
used to store things on

shell (n)
shells
a hard, natural covering. Nuts, eggs
and some animals, such as snails,
have shells

shine (v)
shines, shining, shone
to give out light or to reflect bright
light

shiny (adj)
bright, reflecting bright light

ship (n)
ships
a large boat that carries people or
goods across the sea

shirt (n)
shirts
clothing for the top half of your
body with buttons and a collar

shiver (v)
shivers, shivering, shivered
to shake because you are cold

shoe (n)
shoes
a covering for your foot, to protect
it when you walk

shop (n)
shops
a place where you can buy things

short (adj)
not very long or not very tall

shorts (n)
trousers that end above the knee

shout (v)
shouts, shouting, shouted
to speak very loudly

show (v)
shows, showing, showed
to let someone look at something or
watch how to do something

show (n)
shows
a performance

shower (n)
showers
1. a spray of water which you stand
under to wash your body
2. rain or snow that falls for a short
time

shy (adj)
feeling nervous or unsure when you
are around others

sick (adj)
ill, not well

side (n)
sides
1. an edge or surface of a solid
object
2. the right- or left-hand part
of something
3. a team in a game

sight (n)
being able to see

sign (n)
signs
1. a way of giving information
without speaking
2. a notice that uses pictures or
words to tell you what to do or
where to go

sign (v)
signs, signing, signed
1. to write your name
2. to give a signal

silent (adj)
not making any sound

a
b
c
d
e
f
g
h
i
j
k
l
m
n
o
p
q
r
s
t
u
v
w
x
y
z

a
b
c
d
e
f
g
h
i
j
k
l
m
n
o
p
q
r
s
t
u
v
w
x
y
z

silly (adj)
1. not making sense
2. funny, ridiculous

silver (n)
a valuable metal often used to make jewellery

similar (adj)
a lot like something else, but not exactly the same

simple (adj)
1. easy, not difficult
2. plain, not decorated

since
1. between then and now
2. because

sing (v)
sings, singing, sang
to make music with your voice, especially with words

sink (n)
sinks
a bowl, usually with a tap, where you can wash things in water

sink (v)
sinks, sinking, sank
to drop down to the bottom of a liquid

size (n)
sizes
how big something is

skate (n)
skates
a boot that allows you to move while your foot is on the ground. A roller skate rolls on wheels. An ice skate has a blade which cuts into the ice

skate (v)
skates, skating, skated
to move on skates

skateboard (n)
skateboards
a board with wheels, which you stand on to move

skeleton (n)
skeletons
all the bones inside the body
(see page 115)

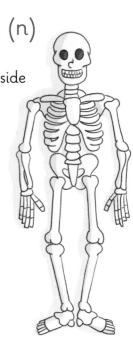

skin (n)

skins

1. the tough layer that covers the outside of the body of people and many animals

2. the tough layer that covers the outside of some fruit and vegetables, such as apples and potatoes

skip (v)

skips, skipping, skipped

1. to move along quickly with a bouncing movement

2. to jump in time to a turning rope

3. to leave something out

skirt (n)

skirts

a piece of clothing worn by girls and women, which hangs from your waist

sky (n)

skies

the huge, open space above the Earth which you see when you look up

sleep (v)

sleeps, sleeping, slept

to close your eyes and not know what is going on around you

slice (n)

slices

a thin piece cut from a bigger thing

slide (n)

slides

a smooth slope, which you can go down for fun

slide (v)

slides, sliding, slid

to move over a smooth surface without taking steps or jumps

slip (v)

slips, slipping, slipped

to slide by mistake

slope (n)

slopes

ground that slants so that one end higher than the other

slow (adj)

not fast, taking a long time to move

small (adj)

little, not big

a b c d e f g h i j k l m n o p q r **s** t u v w x y z

a
b
c
d
e
f
g
h
i
j
k
l
m
n
o
p
q
r
s
t
u
v
w
x
y
z

smartphone (n)

smartphones
a mobile phone that is also a computer and can connect to the internet

smell (n)

smells
the sense of something that reaches you through your nose

smell (v)

smells, smelling, smelt
to sense something through your nose

smile (v)

smiles, smiling, smiled
to pull your lips wide to show that you are happy or to be friendly

smoke (n)

a black, white or grey cloud that rises up from a fire

smooth (adj)

not bumpy or rough

sneeze (n)

sneezes
a blast of air that leaves your body through your nose

sniff (v)

sniffs, sniffing, sniffed
to pull extra air in through your nose

snow (n)

white flakes made of tiny droplets of ice which fall from the sky

soap (n)

something used to clean your skin when mixed with water

sock (n)

socks
a soft covering for the foot

sofa (n)

sofas
a long, soft seat for two or more people. Also known as a settee or couch

soft (adj)

easy to squeeze, not hard

soil (n)
a crumbly, black-and-brown layer covering the Earth, which plants grow in

some
a few, not all
⚠ *sum*

sometimes
not always

song (n)
songs
music with words

soon
in or after a short amount of time

sore (adj)
painful

sorry (adj)
wishing you had not done something

sort (v)
sorts, sorting, sorted
to put things into groups to show how they are alike or different

sound (n)
sounds
something you can hear

soup (n)
soups
liquid food made from vegetables, water and perhaps meat or fish

sour (adj)
tasting sharp and tangy, like lemon juice or vinegar

sow (v)
sows, sowing, sowed
to put seeds into the ground so they will grow
⚠ *sew, so*

space (n)
1. **spaces**
an empty place
2. everything that is farther from Earth than the air

space station (n)
space stations
something built in space for astronauts to live and work in

a
b
c
d
e
f
g
h
i
j
k
l
m
n
o
p
q
r
s
t
u
v
w
x
y
z

spacecraft (n)

a vehicle that travels into space

spade (n)

spades

a long tool with a flat end, used for digging

speak (v)

speaks, speaking, spoke

to say something

special (adj)

1. better than usual

2. made for a particular purpose. For example, you use a special brush to clean your teeth

speed (n)

speeds

how fast something moves

spell (n)

spells

in stories, words and actions that make magic happen

spell (v)

spells, spelling, spelt

to put letters in the right order to make a particular word

spend (v)

spends, spending, spent

1. to use money to buy something

2. to use time to do something

spider (n)

spiders

a small animal with eight legs

(see page 126)

spill (v)

spills, spilling, spilt

to let liquid escape by mistake

splash (v)

splashes, splashing, splashed

to make large drops of water or other liquid jump into the air

spoil (v)

spoils, spoiling, spoilt

1. to damage something or to make it not so good

2. to give a child too many toys or not enough rules

sponge (n)

sponges

1. a kind of cake
2. a big group of connected threads that form the skeleton of some sea animals
3. a material full of small holes, which absorbs water and is used for cleaning

spoon (n)

spoons

a tool used for eating, with a small bowl on the end of a long handle

sport (n)

sports

games and activities, such as running and jumping, which you do for exercise, for fun and to compete with other people

spot (n)

spots

a small, round mark

spot (v)

spots, spotting, spotted

to notice something

square (n)

squares

a shape with four even sides
(see page 118)

squash (v)

squashes, squashing, squashed

to press flat

squeeze (v)

squeezes, squeezing, squeezed

to press from both sides

stairs (n)

a set of steps that join a lower floor to a higher floor

⚠ *stares*

stamp (n)

stamps

1. a small piece of paper that you stick on an envelope or parcel to show you have paid for the letter or parcel to be delivered

Little Red Hen
5 Acorn Road
Brambly Village
Fairyland

2. an object you dip in ink then press on to paper to make a word or mark

stamp (v)

stamps, stamping, stamped

to bang your foot loudly on the floor

a b c d e f g h i j k l m n o p q r **s** t u v w x y z

a
b
c
d
e
f
g
h
i
j
k
l
m
n
o
p
q
r
s
t
u
v
w
x
y
z

stand (v)

stands, standing, stood
to be upright on your feet without moving

star (n)

stars
1. a huge, heavy mass of burning gas in space. From Earth, it looks like a tiny point of light in the night sky
2. a person who is famous

star (v)

stars, starring, starred
to be the most important actor in a play or film

stare (v)

stares, staring, stared
to look hard at something for a long time
⚠ *stairs*

start (v)

starts, starting, started
to begin

station (n)

stations
1. a place where trains or buses stop and people can get on and off
2. the building where firefighters or police officers are based

stay (v)

stays, staying, stayed
1. to not move from a place
2. to live somewhere for a short time. You might stay somewhere for a holiday

steady (adj)

not wobbling or shaking

steal (v)

steals, stealing, stole
to take something that does not belong to you

steam (n)

the cloud of tiny water droplets that forms above hot water

steep (adj)

almost straight up

steer (v)

steers, steering, steered
to control which way a vehicle goes

stem (n)

stems
The main body or stalk of a plant
(see page 127)

step (n)

steps
1. the distance between one foot and the other when you walk
2. a flat strip or piece of ground, which is built a bit higher than the strip or ground below it

step (v)

steps, stepping, stepped
to move one foot away from the other and put your weight on to it

stick (n)

sticks
a long, thin piece of wood

stick (v)

sticks, sticking, stuck
to glue one thing to another

still (adj)

not moving

sting (v)

stings, stinging, stung
1. to make you feel a sharp pain
2. to push a poisonous substance into the skin, for example from a bee

stir (v)

stirs, stirring, stirred
to mix different things together by moving them around with a spoon or other tool

stone (n)

stones
1. a small piece of rock
(see page 128)
2. a hard seed in the centre of some fruit

stop (v)

stops, stopping, stopped
to finish moving or doing something

store (n)

stores
1. things kept to use in future
2. a shop

store (v)

stores, storing, stored
to keep something to use in the future

a
b
c
d
e
f
g
h
i
j
k
l
m
n
o
p
q
r
s
t
u
v
w
x
y
z

storm

b
c
d
e
f
g
h
i
j
k
l
m
n
o
p
q
r
s
t
u
v
w
x
y
z

storm (n)

storms

very bad weather with strong wind, heavy rain or snow, and perhaps thunder and lightning

story (n)

stories

words describing something that has happened, or something made up, for entertainment

straight (adj)

not bent

strange (adj)

unusual, or unlike what you know already

stranger (n)

strangers

a person you do not know

straw (n)

straws

1. a thin tube used to suck up a drink
2. the stems of cut wheat or corn

stream (n)

streams

a small river

street (n)

streets

a road with houses, shops and other buildings on it

strength (n)

how strong something or someone is

stretch (v)

stretches, stretching, stretched

to make something longer by pulling both ends

string (n)

a long, thin piece of material used to tie things

stripe (n)

stripes

a band of colour

stroke (v)

strokes, stroking, stroked

to move your hand gently across something

strong (adj)

1. not easily broken, or able to take or lift a heavy weight
2. a lot of smell or taste. Food has a strong taste when it has a lot of flavour

submarine (n)

submarines

a type of boat that travels under the water

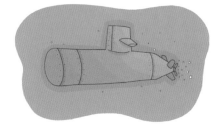

suck (v)

sucks, sucking, sucked

to pull something into your mouth with your lips and tongue

sudden (adj)

happening quickly without warning

sugar (n)

sugars

(say *shuga*) tiny crystals found in some plants and used to sweeten food

sum (n)

sums

adding, subtracting, multiplying or dividing two or more numbers to find the answer

⚠ *some*

summer (n)

summers

a season of the year
(see page 121)

Sun (n)

a star that the Earth travels round and which gives us light and heat

supermarket (n)

supermarkets

a large shop that sells many types of food and some other things

sure (adj)

to have no doubt

surface (n)

surfaces

the outside layer of something

surname (n)

surnames

your family name

surprise (n)

surprises

something you do not expect

swallow (v)

swallows, swallowing, swallowed

to move food from your mouth into your throat

sweat (n)

(say *swet*) salty liquid that comes from your skin when you are very hot and cools you down

a
b
c
d
e
f
g
h
i
j
k
l
m
n
o
p
q
r
s
t
u
v
w
x
y
z

a
b
c
d
e
f
g
h
i
j
k
l
m
n
o
p
q
r
s
t
u
v
w
x
y
z

sweet (n)

sweets

a small treat made with sugar

sweet (adj)

1. having a strong taste of sugar
2. very nice

swim (v)

swims, swimming, swam

to move through the water with your feet off the ground

swing (v)

swings, swinging, swung

to move backwards and forward through the air

switch (n)

switches

part of a machine that turns it on or off

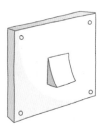

sword (n)

swords

(say *sord*) a long, metal blade with a handle, used for fighting

synagogue (n)

synagogues

(say *sin-a-gog*) a building where Jews meet to pray

Tt

table (n)

tables

a piece of furniture with legs and a flat top, made to put things on

tablet (n)

tablets

1. a pill or small object containing medicine, which you swallow
2. a small computer, halfway in size between a laptop and a smartphone

tail (n)

tails

a long bony part that begins at the bottom of the back of some animals

⚠ *tale*

take (v)

takes, taking, took

1. to carry something with you
2. to get and hold on to something

tale (n)

tales

a story

⚠ *tail*

talk (v)

talks, talking, talked

to speak

tall (adj)

reaching high from the ground

tame (adj)

an animal that is used to being with people and will not harm them

tape (n)

tapes

1. a thin strip of cloth

2. a paper or plastic strip that is sticky on one side

taste (n)

tastes

how sweet, salty, sour or bitter food is in your mouth

tea (n)

1. a drink made from boiling water poured on to tea leaves

2. a meal with bread and cakes which is eaten at the end of the afternoon or in the early evening

teach (v)

teaches, teaching, taught

to help people by giving them information or by showing them how to do things

team (n)

teams

a group of people who play on the same side in a game, or who work together

tear (n)

tears

(say *teer*) a drop of liquid that flows out of your eye when you cry

tear (v)

tears, tearing, tore

(say *tare*) to rip paper or other material

tease (v)

teases, teasing, teased

to make fun of someone

telephone (n)

telephones

a machine that allows you to speak to someone far away

a b c d e f g h i j k l m n o p q r s t u v w x y z

a
b
c
d
e
f
g
h
i
j
k
l
m
n
o
p
q
r
s
t
u
v
w
x
y
z

television (n)
televisions
a machine that shows pictures and sounds for people to watch and listen to

tell (v)
tells, telling, told
to speak to someone to give them information

temperature (n)
temperatures
how hot or cold something is

temple (n)
temples
a building where people who share a religion meet. Hindus, Sikhs and many other faiths have their own temples

tent (n)
tents
a shelter made of fabric and poles

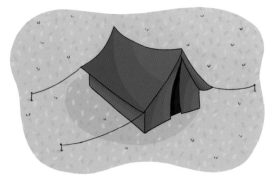

terrible (adj)
very bad or unpleasant

test (n)
tests
questions or activities to see how much someone knows or can do

test (v)
tests, testing, tested
1. to try something out
2. to find out how much someone knows or can do

thank (v)
thanks, thanking, thanked
to tell someone that you are grateful for something they have done or given you

theatre (n)

theatres

a place where you can see plays
or shows

their

belonging to them

thermometer (n)

thermometers

something that measures
temperature

thick (adj)

wide, measuring a long way across

thief (n)

thieves

a person who steals something

thin (adj)

1. narrow, measuring a short way
across
2. not having much fat on your body

thing (n)

things

an object that can be touched or seen

think (v)

thinks, thinking, thought

1. to use your mind
2. to believe that something is so

thirsty (adj)

needing to drink

thought (n)

thoughts

words and pictures in your mind

through

passing along or across the middle
of something
⚠ *threw*

throw (v)

throws, throwing, threw

to move your arm and let go of
something in your hand to send it
through the air

thumb (n)

thumbs

the short, strong finger at the side
of your hand *(see page 114)*

thunder (n)

a loud rumble in the sky caused by
vibrations in the air after a flash
of lightning

ticket (n)
tickets
a piece of paper that shows you have paid for a journey or to see an event or show

tickle (n)
tickles
a light touch on the skin that feels funny or uncomfortable but not painful. Being tickled a lot makes you laugh

tidy (adj)
neat, when everything is in the correct place

tie (n)
ties
1. a thin strip of material that is tied in a special knot round the neck
2. when two people or teams have an equal score at the end of a game

tie (v)
ties, tying, tied
to make a knot to hold two strips of material together, such as shoelaces

tight (adj)
pulled close, not loose

time (n)
1. a moment of a day measured in hours, minutes and seconds
2. how long something lasts

tin (n)
tins
1. a metal container. Food such as soup is sold in airtight tins to keep it fresh
2. a type of metal

tired (adj)
needing to sleep or rest

tissue (n)
tissues
soft paper, often used to wipe your nose

title (n)
titles
the name of a book, film or song

toast (n)
bread that has been grilled to make it crisp and brown

toast (v)
toasts, toasting, toasted
to grill food until its surface is brown – especially bread

today (n)
this day

together
with another person or other people

toilet (n)
toilets
1. a bowl that collects human waste
2. a small room with a toilet

tomorrow (n)
the day after this one

tongue (n)
tongues
a bendy mass of muscle inside your mouth, which you use for eating and speaking *(see page 115)*

tonight (n)
the night that follows today

tool (n)
tools
something you use to help you do a particular job

tooth (n)
teeth
a hard, white object in your mouth, which you use to bite and to chew. Children have twenty teeth and adults have thirty-two

top (n)
tops
1. the highest part of something *(see page 110)*
2. the lid of a bottle, tube, pen or similar object
3. clothing that you wear on your upper body, such as a T-shirt

touch (v)
touches, touching, touched
to feel something with your hand or other part of your body

towel (n)
towels
a rectangle of thick cloth used to dry yourself

town (n)
towns
a place with many buildings, including homes, shops and offices

a b c d e f g h i j k l m n o p q r s **t** u v w x y z

a
b
c
d
e
f
g
h
i
j
k
l
m
n
o
p
q
r
s
t
u
v
w
x
y
z

toy (n)
toys
something that children play with

traffic (n)
all the vehicles travelling on a road

train (n)
trains
a vehicle that moves along railway lines *(see page 116)*

trainer (n)
trainers
a type of shoe with a thick sole, which is good for running around and playing sport

translucent (adj)
partly see-through

transparent (adj)
completely see-through

tree (n)
trees
a tall plant with a wooden stem called a trunk, with branches and leaves growing from it
(see page 127)

trick (n)
tricks
1. something that misleads people for fun
2. a clever thing you have learnt, such as walking on your hands

trouble (n)
troubles
something that makes things difficult or unpleasant

trousers (n)
clothing that goes from your waist to your ankles, with a separate part for each leg

true (adj)
something that is a fact

try (v)
tries, trying, tried
to have a go

T-shirt (n)
T-shirts
clothing with short sleeves worn on the upper body

tube (n)
tubes
1. a thin pipe
2. a container for paste, such as toothpaste

tumble (v)
tumbles, tumbling, tumbled
to fall over

tune (n)
tunes
musical notes in a pattern, which are played or sung one after the other

tunnel (n)
tunnels
a passage through a hill or under the ground

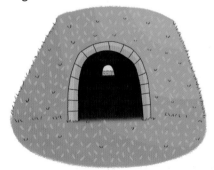

turn (n)
turns
when one person at a time does something

turn (v)
turns, turning, turned
to move round in a circle or to change direction

twice
two times

twig (n)
twigs
a piece of wood growing from a branch

twin (n)
twins
one of two children born to the same mother

twist (v)
twists, twisting, twisted
to turn something round itself or round something else

tyre (n)
tyres
a circle of tough rubber that covers the wheel of a vehicle

a
b
c
d
e
f
g
h
i
j
k
l
m
n
o
p
q
r
s
t
u
v
w
x
y
z

a
b
c
d
e
f
g
h
i
j
k
l
m
n
o
p
q
r
s
t
u
v
w
x
y
z

Uu

ugly (adj)
not nice to look at

umbrella (n)
umbrellas
an object that you hold over your head to keep you dry in the rain

understand (v)
understands, understanding, understood
to know what something means

undo (v)
undoes, undoing, undid
to put something back to the way it was

undress (v)
undresses, undressing, undressed
to take off your clothes

uniform (n)
uniforms
clothes worn to show that someone belongs to a particular school or does a particular job

until
up to the time that

unusual (adj)
not happening very often

upset (adj)
unhappy, sad or cross

upside down (adj)
when the bottom is at the top and the top is at the bottom

upstairs (adj)
on a higher floor of the same building

use (v)
uses, using, used
to do something with the help of a particular thing

useful (adj)
able to be helpful

usual (adj)
what happens most often

Vv

vacuum cleaner (n)
vacuum cleaners
an electrical machine that sucks up dirt

valley (n)
valleys
low land between two hills or mountains

valuable (adj)
of great value or importance

value (n)
values
1. the amount of money something is worth
2. how important something is

vanish (v)
vanishes, vanishing, vanished
to disappear

vase (n)
vases
a tall container for holding flowers

vegetable (n)
vegetables
any part of a plant, except the fruit, that is eaten as food *(see page 113)*

vegetarian (n)
vegetarians
a person who does not eat meat or fish

vehicle (n)
vehicles
something that is used to carry people or things from one place to another *(see page 116)*

very (adj)
a lot, a large amount

vet (n)
vets
a doctor who takes care of sick or injured animals

view (n)
views
1. what you can see in front of you, especially a piece of beautiful scenery
2. what you think about something

a
b
c
d
e
f
g
h
i
j
k
l
m
n
o
p
q
r
s
t
u
v
w
x
y
z

a
b
c
d
e
f
g
h
i
j
k
l
m
n
o
p
q
r
s
t
u
v
w
x
y
z

village (n)

villages

a group of houses and other buildings. A village is smaller than a town

visit (v)

visits, visiting, visited

to go to see someone or something

voice (n)

voices

the sounds you make when you speak or sing

volcano (n)

volcanoes

a mountain with a big hole in the top where hot rocks and gas sometimes shoot out from deep inside the Earth

vowel (n)

vowels

one of the letters A, E, I, O or U

Ww

wait (v)

waits, waiting, waited

to stay somewhere or not do anything until something you are expecting happens

⚠ *weight*

wake (v)

wakes, waking, woke

to stop sleeping

walk (v)

walks, walking, walked

to move along by putting one foot in front of the other

wall (n)

walls

1. the side of a building or room

2. bricks or stones built up round the edge of a garden or other outside space

want (v)

wants, wanting, wanted

to feel you would like to have something or do something

wardrobe (n)

wardrobes

a cupboard with space to hang clothes

warm (adj)

between hot and cold

wash (v)

washes, washing, washed

to use soap and water to make something clean

waste (n)

wastes

something left over that is thrown away

waste (v)

wastes, wasting, wasted

1. to throw something out before it has been used
2. to use more of something than you need

watch (n)

watches

a small clock that you attach to your wrist with a strap

watch (v)

watches, watching, watched

to look at something or someone for a while

water (n)

waters

a clear liquid that falls from the sky as rain and which we need to drink to stay alive

waterproof (adj)

not allowing water to pass through. A waterproof coat keeps you dry when it rains

wave (n)

waves

when the wind blows the surface of a liquid into very large ripples

wave (v)

waves, waving, waved

to move your hand back and forth in the air as a greeting or to get someone's attention

a
b
c
d
e
f
g
h
i
j
k
l
m
n
o
p
q
r
s
t
u
v
w
x
y
z

a
b
c
d
e
f
g
h
i
j
k
l
m
n
o
p
q
r
s
t
u
v
w
x
y
z

way (n)

ways

1. how to do something

2. the path or route from one place to another

⚠ *weigh*

weak (adj)

not strong, easily broken

⚠ *week*

wear (v)

wears, wearing, wore

to have on your body. For example, clothes or jewellery

weather (n)

what is happening in the air outside. Weather includes rain, sunshine, wind and snow, as well as how hot or cold the air is

website (n)

websites

a place on the internet that contains information about a particular subject

week (n)

weeks

seven days and nights *(see page 117)*

⚠ *weak*

weigh (v)

weighs, weighing, weighed

to find out how heavy something is *(see page 120)*

⚠ *way*

weight (n)

weights

how heavy something is

⚠ *wait*

well (n)

wells

a place where water or oil is brought to the surface from deep below the ground

well (adj)

not ill

wet (adj)

not dry, covered with a layer of water or full of water

wheat (n)

a plant grown by farmers. The grains (seeds) of wheat are made into flour

wheel (n)

wheels

a round object that turns.
Cars, bicycles and other vehicles
have wheels that turn to move
them along

while

during the time that. For example,
'I play the piano while she sings.'

while (n)

a period of time. For example,
'I'm going out for a while.'

whisper (v)

whispers, whispering, whispered

to speak very quietly

whistle (n)

whistles

(say *wissle*) a small tube that you
blow through to make a loud, high
sound

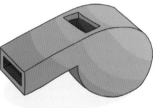

whistle (v)

whistles, whistling, whistled

to make a loud, high sound by
blowing through your lips

whole (adj)

(say *hole*) all of something

⚠ *hole*

wide (adj)

a long way from side to side

wild (adj)

not tamed or looked after by people

win (v)

wins, winning, won

to come first in a race or competition

wind (n)

winds

air that moves fast

wind (v)

winds, winding, wound

(say *wynd*)

1. to twist something round
and round

2. to take a twisting and
turning route

window (n)

windows

an opening in the wall of a building
or vehicle which lets in light

a
b
c
d
e
f
g
h
i
j
k
l
m
n
o
p
q
r
s
t
u
v
w
x
y
z

wing (n)

wings

the part of the body of a bird, insect or bat that it uses to fly. Aircraft also have wings

wire (n)

wires

a long, thin piece of metal which bends easily

wish (v)

wishes, wishing, wished

to want something to happen

witch (n)

witches

in stories, a woman who can do magic

without

not have something or not do something

wizard (n)

wizards

in stories, a man who can do magic

woman (n)

women

a grown-up female

wonder (n)

wonders

the feeling when something is amazing, surprising or beautiful

wonder (v)

wonders, wondering, wondered

to think about something you do not know

wonderful (adj)

amazing

wood (n)

woods

1. a place where many trees grow close together

2. a material that comes from trees *(see page 128)*

wool (n)

1. the coat of a sheep and some other animals

2. a material made by spinning the wool from those animals

word (n)

words

a group of letters with a particular
meaning

work (n)

1. something that takes time
or effort
2. a job that someone is paid to do

work (v)

works, working, worked

1. to do something that takes effort
or that you get paid for
2. if a machine works, it does what
it is meant to do

world (n)

worlds

a particular place and everything
in it

world wide web (n)

part of the internet that allows you
to get information stored on
computers all over the world

worm (n)

worms

a type of animal with no bones
and no legs, which slithers
along the ground

worry (v)

worries, worrying, worried

to be concerned that something bad
might happen

worse (adj)

not as good as before, or as
something else

worst (adj)

the least good thing of all

wriggle (v)

wriggles, wriggling, wriggled

to twist quickly from side to side

write (v)

writes, writing, wrote

to put words on paper

⚠ *right*

wrong (adj)

not right

a
b
c
d
e
f
g
h
i
j
k
l
m
n
o
p
q
r
s
t
u
v
w
x
y
z

Xx

X-ray (n)

X-rays
a type of photograph of the bones inside the body

xylophone (n)

xylophones
(say *zylo-fone*) an instrument that makes musical notes when strips of wood are hit by sticks

Yy

yacht (n)

yachts
(say *yot*) a boat with sails

yawn (v)

yawns, yawning, yawned
to take a big breath of air in through your mouth when you are tired or bored

year (n)

years
the time it takes for twelve months to pass

yesterday (n)

the day before this day

yoghurt (n)

yoghurts
a type of thick, runny food made from milk and, often, fruit

young (adj)

not old, not yet grown-up, or recently grown-up

a
b
c
d
e
f
g
h
i
j
k
l
m
n
o
p
q
r
s
t
u
v
w
x
y
z

Zz

zero (n)
zeros
the number written as 0, nothing

zigzag (n)
zigzags
a pattern of lines that looks like
many letter Zs joined together

zip (n)
zips
two strips of metal or plastic teeth
that lock together to fasten clothes,
bags and other things

zoo (n)
zoos
a place where wild animals are kept
to protect them and so that people
can go and see them

a
b
c
d
e
f
g
h
i
j
k
l
m
n
o
p
q
r
s
t
u
v
w
x
y
z

Grammar

Noun (n)

A noun is a naming word. You can tell a noun by whether you can put the word 'the' or 'a' in front of it. Some nouns are things you can touch:

tree   school

glove   door

Some are things you cannot touch:

week   trouble

sound   language

Proper noun

A proper noun is the name of a person or place. It begins with a capital letter:

Anna   Tony

London   Australia

Adjective (adj)

An adjective describes a noun:

big   soft

scary   happy

pretty   tall

old   shiny

Verb (v)

A verb is a doing or being word:

act   drink

look   talk

jump   write

swim   read

Most verbs have these endings:

walk: walk**s**, walk**ing**, walk**ed**

dance: dan**ces**, danc**ing**, danc**ed**

Some verbs have different
endings:

be: is, being, was

buy: buys, buying, bought

carry: carries, carrying,
carried

come: comes, coming, came

do: does, doing, did

get: gets, getting, got

give: gives, giving, gave

go: goes, going, went

have: has, having, had

run: runs, running, ran

say: says, saying, said

see: sees, seeing, saw

sit: sits, sitting, sat

take: takes, taking, took

Adverb

An adverb describes a verb.
Most adverbs end in 'ly':

quickly   nicely
smoothly   tightly

But some adverbs do not
end in 'ly':

soon   enough
fast   again

Question words

Use these words to ask a
question:

who?   when?
where?   which?
what?   how?
why?   whose?

Connective words

These words are sometimes called
conjunctions. Use them to join two
sentences together:

and   but
because   so

Common words

People words

I, me, my

you, your

we, us, our

he, him, his

she, her

they, them, their

father, dad

mother, mum

brother

sister

grandpa, grandad, grandfather

grandma, granny, grandmother

grandson, granddaughter, grandchild

aunt, uncle, cousin, niece, nephew

friend

Opposites

above	below
back	front
before	after
begin	end
in	out
inside	outside
left	right
over	under
push	pull
shallow	deep
top	bottom
up	down

Colours

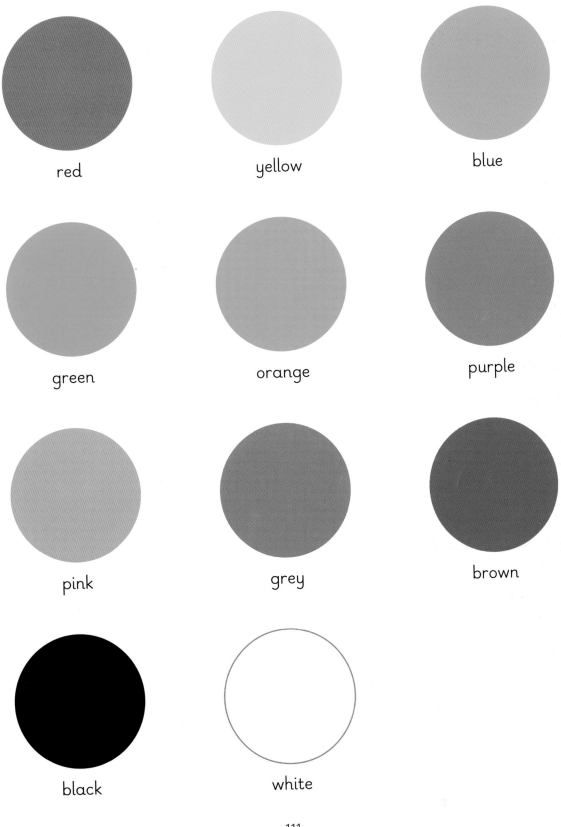

red

yellow

blue

green

orange

purple

pink

grey

brown

black

white

Fruit

apple

banana

blueberry

kiwi fruit

lemon

melon

orange

peach

pear

pineapple

plum

raspberry

strawberry

tomato

Vegetables

aubergine

bean

broccoli

cabbage

carrot

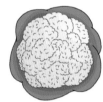

cauliflower

cucumber

leek

lettuce

onion

pea

potato

sweetcorn

turnip

The body

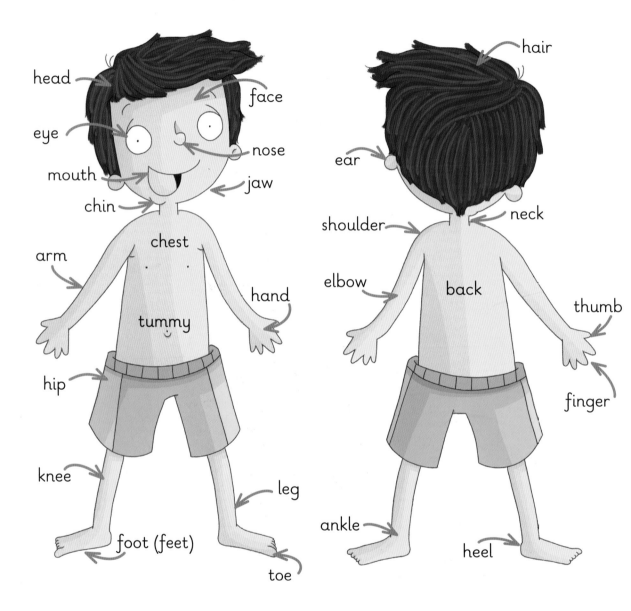

head
face
eye
nose
mouth
jaw
chin
chest
arm
hand
tummy
hip
knee
leg
foot (feet)
toe

hair
ear
neck
shoulder
elbow
back
thumb
finger
ankle
heel

Outside

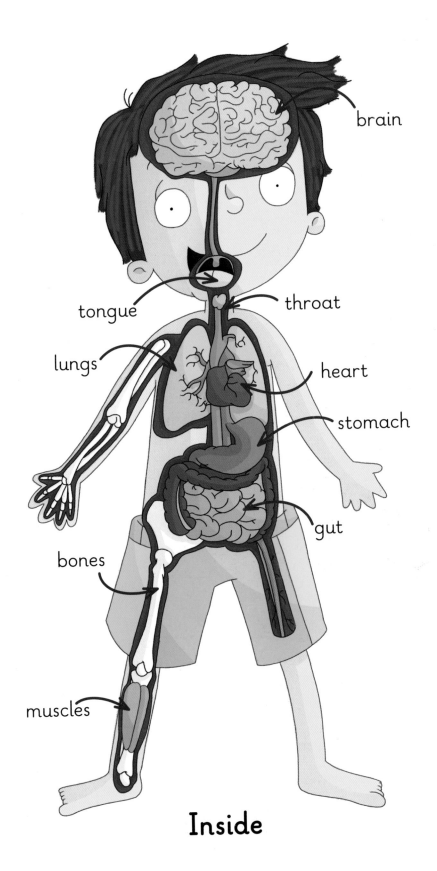

brain

tongue

throat

lungs

heart

stomach

gut

bones

muscles

Inside

Vehicles

Vehicles carry people or goods from one place to another.

aeroplane

ambulance

bicycle

boat

bus

car

fire engine

lorry

motorbike

tractor

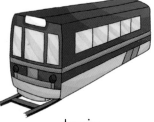

train

van

Days of the week

Monday
Tuesday
Wednesday
Thursday
Friday
Saturday
Sunday

Months of the year

January
February
March
April
May
June
July
August
September
October
November
December

Maths words

Shapes

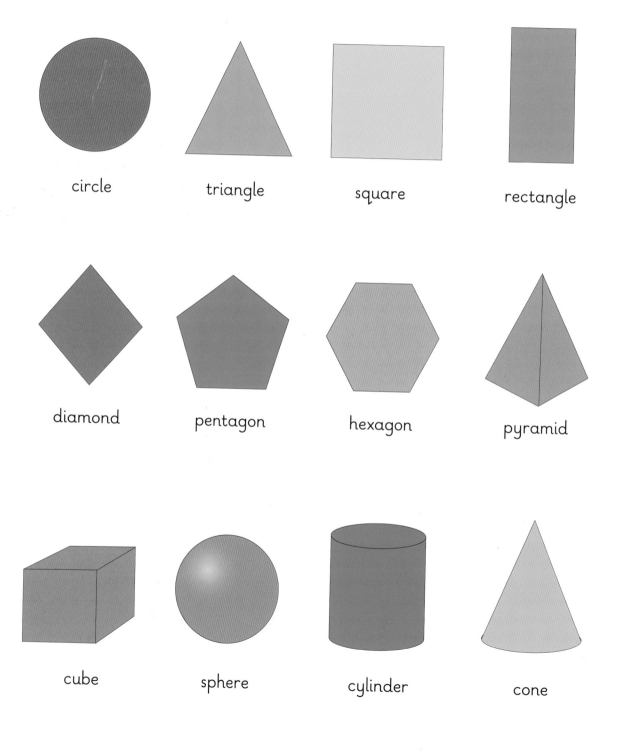

circle

triangle

square

rectangle

diamond

pentagon

hexagon

pyramid

cube

sphere

cylinder

cone

Cardinal numbers

1	one	11	eleven	30	thirty
2	two	12	twelve	40	forty
3	three	13	thirteen	50	fifty
4	four	14	fourteen	60	sixty
5	five	15	fifteen	70	seventy
6	six	16	sixteen	80	eighty
7	seven	17	seventeen	90	ninety
8	eight	18	eighteen	100	one hundred
9	nine	19	nineteen	1,000	one thousand
10	ten	20	twenty	1,000,000	one million

Ordinal numbers

1st	first	11th	eleventh
2nd	second	12th	twelfth
3rd	third	20th	twentieth
4th	fourth	100th	hundredth
5th	fifth	1,000th	thousandth
6th	sixth		
7th	seventh		
8th	eighth		
9th	ninth		
10th	tenth		

Odd numbers: 1, 3, 5, 7, 9 …
Even numbers: 2, 4, 6, 8, 10 …

Measuring

Length or height

millimetre (mm)

centimetre (cm)

metre (m)

kilometre (km)

10 mm = 1 cm

100 cm = 1 m

1,000 m = 1 km

Weight

gram (g)

kilogram (kg)

1,000 g = 1 kg

Capacity

millilitre (ml)

litre (l)

1,000 ml = 1 l

Science words

Seasons

spring

summer

autumn

winter

Animals

Herbivores

Herbivores eat plants.

Carnivores

Carnivores eat other animals.

Omnivores

Omnivores eat plants and animals.

Scavengers

Scavengers eat the remains of plants and animals.

Mammals

Mammals have hair or fur. Mammal mothers feed their babies with their own milk.

bear

cat

cow

monkey

mouse

panda

pig

seal

sheep

tiger

whale

zebra

Birds

Birds have feathers and wings. Not all birds can fly.

hen

mallard duck

ostrich

owl

Amphibians

Amphibians spend part of their lives in water and part on land.

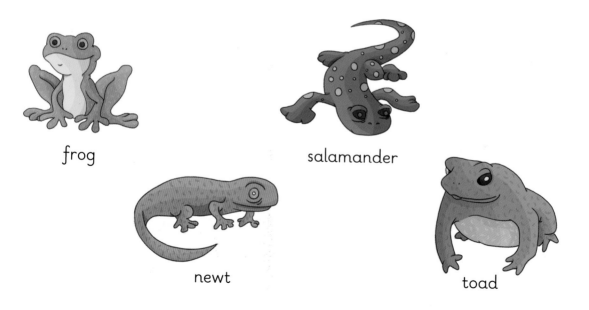

frog

salamander

newt

toad

Fish

Fish live in water and have fins.

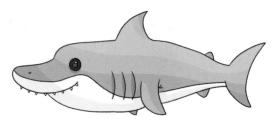

cod

shark

goldfish

tuna

Reptiles

Reptiles have dry skin covered with scales.

crocodile

lizard

snake

turtle

Invertebrates

Invertebrates have no bones inside their bodies.

crab

jellyfish

octopus

snail

spider

worm

Insects are invertebrates. They have six legs and their bodies are divided into three parts.

ant

bee

butterfly

fly

ladybird

Plants

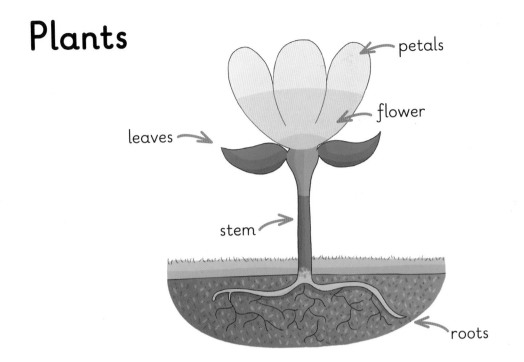

petals

flower

leaves

stem

roots

Trees

deciduous tree

For example, apple or oak trees.
These lose their leaves in autumn.

evergreen tree

For example, pine or fir trees.
These have leaves or needles
all year round.

Materials

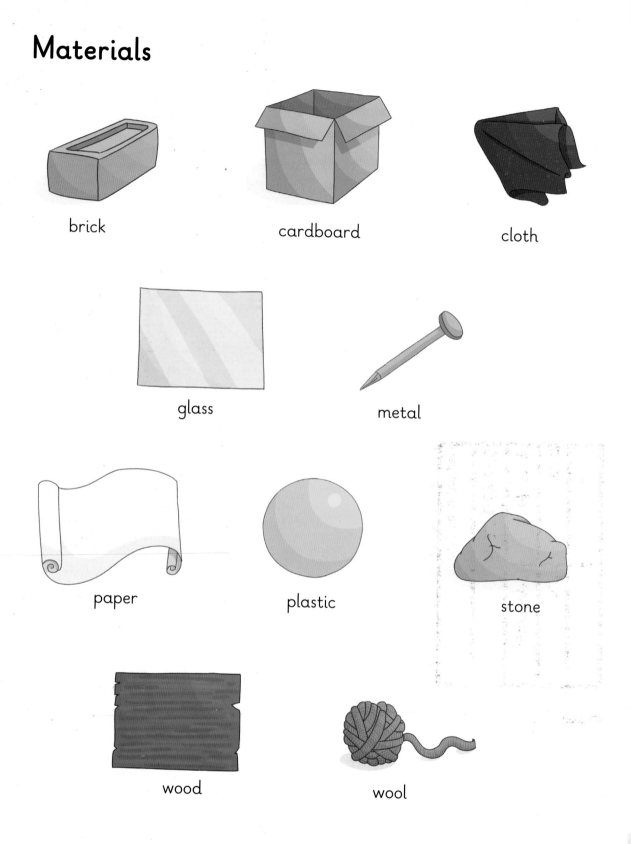

brick

cardboard

cloth

glass

metal

paper

plastic

stone

wood

wool